EFFECTIVE WRITING
A PRACTICAL GRAMMAR REVIEW

EFFECTIVE WRITING
A PRACTICAL GRAMMAR REVIEW

THIRD EDITION

Ted D. Stoddard
Max L. Waters
R. DerMont Bell
Devern J. Perry
All of Brigham Young University

IRWIN

Chicago • Bogota • Boston • Buenos Aires • Caracas
London • Madrid • Mexico City • Sydney • Toronto

Senior sponsoring editor: Craig Beytien
Editorial assistant: Jennifer R. McBride
Senior marketing manager: Kurt Messersmith
Project editor: Paula M. Buschman
Production manager: Pat Frederickson
Designer: Mercedes Santos
Printer: Malloy Lithographing, Inc.

Library of Congress Cataloging-in-Publication Data

Effective writing : a practical grammar review / Ted D. Stoddard . . .
   [et al.]. — 3rd ed.
    p.   cm.
   Includes index.
   ISBN 0-256-14153-3
    1. English language—Rhetoric.   2. English language—Grammar.
  I. Stoddard, Ted D.
  PE1408.E355   1995
  808'.042—dc20   94–25369

Printed in the United States of America
2 3 4 5 6 7 8 9 0 ML 1 0 9 8 7 6 5

PREFACE

Good writing skills can be an asset to almost everyone. Writing skills are especially valuable in any discipline in which the ability to communicate clearly is vital. In fact, the ability to write well is one of the most-important skills people in all walks of life can possess.

An understanding of practical English grammar is an advantage to any writer. Although successful writers are not necessarily grammar experts, they understand grammar well enough to make its proper use a valuable writing tool.

The third edition of *Effective Writing: A Practical Grammar Review* is designed to strengthen your writing skills. It provides a concentrated review of key usage principles, rules, and concepts. Readable and easy-to-understand discussions of grammar principles are accompanied by rules of usage and helpful illustrations of how these principles should be applied. *Practical Grammar Review* is not a comprehensive grammar textbook. Instead, it concentrates on the most frequently used and abused principles, rules, and concepts of grammar usage.

Each chapter of *Practical Grammar Review* is independent of the others. Therefore, you can study the chapters in any order you desire. In a few instances, rules are duplicated in more than one chapter. However, such duplication is minimal but also necessary to make each chapter independent of the others.

Useful "do's and don'ts" called *learning tips* are included to help you apply these important grammar principles, rules, and concepts correctly. In addition, a variety of application exercises that provide further opportunities for review and reinforcement accompany each chapter. Finally, the computer-assisted instruction that accompanies *Practical Grammar Review* provides a distinctive medium for reinforcing the principles, rules, and concepts.

In summary, the major components of each chapter of *Practical Grammar Review* are as follows:

- A background discussion section
- The terminology for the chapter
- The rules for the chapter
- A self-evaluation exercise
- The application exercises
- Rule-driven computer-assisted instruction

As you study *Practical Grammar Review*, read carefully the discussion that introduces each chapter. Next, review the terminology and try to understand each term. Then, pay close attention to the rules of usage that follow. The rules emphasize the most-common (and the most-important) applications of each grammar principle reviewed.

The illustrations and the learning tips will be especially helpful. They explain and clarify; and they will help you see more clearly how the grammar principles can be used correctly to make you a better writer.

When the discussion, terminology, and rules in each chapter have been studied carefully, use the practice exercises at the end of the chapter to check your understanding. Eight exercises are provided for each chapter. Use all of them or some of them—as you wish or as directed by your instructor or supervisor.

The practice exercises should be an important part of your review. They can help you identify your strengths and weaknesses in understanding key principles and concepts. They also provide additional opportunities for learning and for reinforcing the principles of grammar usage you will study in *Practical Grammar Review*.

Note that each chapter includes a self-evaluation exercise with an accompanying key to help you determine how well you understand the material just reviewed. Keys for the other practice exercises at the end of each chapter are provided in the instructor's manual.

Most students and other writers know more about grammar than they realize. Often, however, they have become rusty in its usage or have forgotten something they once knew. *Practical Grammar Review* provides a realistic review for those who need one and does so in an easy-to-read and understandable way.

Study *Practical Grammar Review* carefully. Your mastery of the material can make you a better writer and a faster writer; and the rewards for good writing are many. Although some writing authorities question the value of studying grammar, we promise you that you will find increased power in your writing skills if you master *Practical Grammar Review*.

CONTENTS

CASE

DISCUSSION

The word *case* is used to describe the property of a noun or pronoun and to show the relationship of the noun or pronoun to other parts of the sentence. English has three cases, as follows:

1. **Subjective case** (sometimes called *nominative* case): Used for the subject or the subject complement (predicate noun or predicate pronoun) of a verb.

    Subject: *He* voted for the proposal.
    Subject complement (predicate pronoun): Marylou is *she*.

2. **Objective case**: Used for (a) the direct or indirect object of a verb; (b) the object of a preposition; (c) the subject of an infinitive; (d) the object of an infinitive; or (e) the complement of the infinitive *to be*.

    Direct object: LeeAnn drove *him* to the airport.
    Indirect object: Robert gave *me* his expense report.
    Object of a preposition: Barbara has not given the keys to *me*.
    Subject of an infinitive: William wants *her* to give the presentation.
    Object of an infinitive: Lila needs to write *him* tomorrow.
    Complement of *to be*: The committee believed me to be *her*.

3. **Possessive case**: Used to show ownership.

    The car is *Sam's*.
    My *boss'* job is complicated.
    The *table's* leg is broken.
    The *managers'* actions are appropriate.
    The decision is *yours*.
    The dog had *its* collar stolen.

Nouns change form for the possessive case only, but pronouns may change form for the subjective, the objective, or the possessive case. To use the correct pronoun, you must know the forms for pronouns, as follows:

Subjective	Objective	Possessive
I	me	my, mine
you	you	your, yours
he, she, it	him, her, it	his, hers, its
we	us	our, ours
they	them	their, theirs
who	whom	whose

TERMINOLOGY

Abstract noun—A noun for which a mental image cannot be readily formed in the mind. (Mental images of concrete nouns such as *tree*, *dog*, and *cat* can easily be formed in the mind.)

We won our *independence* with great *difficulty*.
Honesty and *integrity* are important personality *traits*.

Antecedent—The noun for which a pronoun substitutes.

The governor took the Jordanelle Dam report with him. (*Governor* is the antecedent of *him*.)

Appositive—A noun or pronoun word or phrase that immediately follows and that restates a preceding noun or pronoun. An appositive functions the same way in the sentence as the noun or pronoun it complements.

Mr. Lewis, our treasurer, will preside. (*Treasurer*, the appositive, restates *Mr. Lewis*.)

Direct object—A sentence complement of an action verb. Direct objects usually answer the questions *whom?* or *what?* about the subject and its verb.

Henry enjoys college. (*College* answers what Henry enjoys.)
Kristine likes Matt. (*Matt* answers whom Kristine likes.)

Gerund—The verb form used as a noun and ending in -*ing*.

Skiing at Snowbird was a thrilling experience.
Did your *performing* at halftime satisfy a teenage dream?
I have a difficult time understanding Ron's *spending* so much money on the lottery.

CASE

Indirect object—A sentence complement of an action verb. Indirect objects precede direct objects and usually answer the questions *for whom?* or *for what?* or *to whom?* or *to what?*

> Tom gave her the computer. (The indirect object *her* answers *to whom* Tom gave the computer.)
> Grandpa bought James a new rifle. (The indirect object *James* answers *for whom* the rifle was bought.)

Infinitive—The verb form introduced by *to*. May be used as a noun, an adjective, or an adverb.

> *To walk* is the all-consuming goal of my daughter.
> Marie asked *to see* my new book.
> We still have two more reports *to write*.
> Henry resigned *to take* a new job in Denver.
> I asked her *to finish* the report on Saturday.

Noun—The name of a person, place, or thing. Nouns often serve as subjects of verbs. Nouns may be either singular or plural and may be common or proper.

> We have 442 *students* at our *school* in *Albuquerque*.

Objective-case pronoun—The form of a pronoun most commonly used as the object of a verb or of a preposition (*me, him, her, us, them, whom*).

> Maxine wants *him* for an assistant.
> Did I address the letter to *him* or *her*?
> For *whom* did you vote in the last election?

Plural possession—The process of showing that something belongs to more than one person or thing. The apostrophe is used to show possession in possessive nouns—but not in possessive pronouns.

> The *girls'* swimming suits arrived yesterday.
> The *men's* and *women's* soccer teams have won every game.
> The decision about new uniforms is *yours*—not *theirs*.

Possessive-case pronoun—The form of a pronoun used to show a person or thing owning or possessing something (*my, mine, your, yours, his, hers, its, our, ours, their, theirs, whose*).

> *Whose* job is in jeopardy?
> The car is *his*, not *mine*.
> When you finish *your* work, please call *my* office.

Predicate adjective—An adjective that follows a state-of-being verb and that is also called a subject complement. A predicate adjective describes the subject in some way.

> Running is *exhilarating*. (*Exhilarating* describes the gerund subject, *running*.)
> I was *honored* to be selected. (*Honored* describes the pronoun subject *I*.)

Predicate noun or pronoun—A noun or pronoun that follows a state-of-being verb and that explains the subject and is identical with the subject. A predicate noun or pronoun names the same thing or person referred to by the subject and requires a subjective-case pronoun. Also called a subject complement.

> Mark Majors is our *office manager*. (*Office manager* refers to *Mark Majors*.)
> The winner of the California trip is *he*. (The pronoun *he* refers to *winner*.)

Prepositional phrase—A group of words consisting of a preposition plus its object and any words that modify the object.

> *Between you and me*, Joan deserves a big raise.
> I will give the book *to them*.
> Mrs. Frazier saved the apple pie *for us*.

Pronoun—A word used to substitute for a noun. Pronouns are classified in different ways. The pronouns in this lesson are classified as *subjective*, *objective*, and *possessive*.

> Subjective: *I, you, he, she, it, we, they, who*
> Objective: *me, you, him, her, it, us, them, whom*
> Possessive: *my, mine, you, yours, his, hers, its, our, ours, their, theirs, whose*

Singular possession—The process of showing that something belongs to a single person or thing or to several persons or things acting in a singular capacity. The apostrophe is used to show possession in possessive nouns—but not in possessive pronouns.

> *Fred's* car is a 1966 Mustang.
> The *cat's* name is Fred.
> The three dogs are *hers*—not *mine*.

State-of-being verb—Verbs that denote existence. Sometimes known as *be verbs*, *being verbs*, or *to be verbs*. The eight state-of-being verbs are *am, is, are, was, were, be, been,* and *being*. They are used to link the subject and its complement (called a *subject complement* in the form of a predicate noun, predicate pronoun, or predicate adjective). State-of-being verbs are also called linking verbs. All eight state-of-being verbs are linking verbs, but not all linking verbs are state-of-being verbs.

> I *am* he.
> The person responsible *is* she.

The committee members *are* they.

Subject complement—A noun, pronoun, or adjective that follows a state-of-being verb. Depending on the part of speech it is, a subject complement may be called a *predicate noun*, a *predicate pronoun*, or a *predicate adjective*.

Steve's horse is a *mare*. (The subject complement is a noun.)
The manager to see is *he*. (The subject complement is a pronoun.)
My sister is *beautiful*. (The subject complement is an adjective.)

Subjective-case pronoun—The form of a pronoun used as a subject of a verb or as a subject complement (*I, he, she, we, they, who*) following a state-of-being verb. Synonymous with *nominative case*. Because *subjective* makes sense as the subject, *subjective* rather than *nominative* is used throughout *Practical Grammar Review*.

Although *we* arrived late, *they* had not yet started the meeting.
Both *he* and *I* want to conduct.
The person in charge is *I*.
The gospel singers at the Freedom Festival are *they*.

Verb—A word used to express action or state of being. Every clause must have a main verb. Sometimes, other verbs serve as helping verbs to help form a *verb phrase*. The main verb is always the last verb in a verb phrase. Throughout *Practical Grammar Review*, verb phrases functioning as verbs are referred to as *verbs*.

Action verbs: *run, jump, sing, swim, examine, accomplish*
State-of-being verbs: *am, is, are, was, were, be, been, being*
Helping verbs: *am, is, are, was, were, be, been, being, have, has, had, may, must, can, might, could, would, should, shall, will, do, does, did*

RULES FOR SUBJECTIVE CASE

1. Use subjective-case nouns or pronouns as subjects of verbs.

He and *she* are the winners. (*He* and *she* are subjects of the verb *are*.)
I am giving the used computer to *whoever* completes the research on time. (*I* is the subject of the verb *am giving*; *whoever* is the subject of the verb *completes*.)

Learning Tip 1: When two pronouns or a pronoun and a noun are joined with *and* to form a compound subject, (1) separate them mentally and then (2) read each pronoun or noun alone in separate sentences as follows:

Jane and me are attending the convention.

becomes

Jane is attending the convention.

Me am attending the convention. (Obviously, the sentence should read *I* am attending the convention.)

Therefore, the sentence should read

Jane and *I* are attending the convention.

If your native language is English, you may find that hearing the word is useful in making the correct choice. However, relying on sound may not always work and should not substitute for knowing the correct rules. See Learning Tip 7 for an excellent way of choosing correctly between subjective and objective case.

Learning Tip 2: The choice between *who* and *whom* and their variations is difficult to hear. Therefore, try the following steps to determine which word choice is correct in a sentence:

Step 1: Eliminate the part of the sentence up to the *who* or *whom* choice.

Give the report to *whoever/whomever* asks for it.

. . . *whoever/whomever* asks for it.

Step 2: Replace *whoever/whomever* with *him*.

Him asks for it.

Step 3: Read the part of the sentence you have not eliminated (arranging the remaining words to sound natural). If the substituted word sounds correct, use *whom* in the original sentence. If the substituted word does not sound correct, use *who* in the original sentence.

He asks for it. (Sounds better than *Him* asks for it.)

Therefore, use *whoever* in the original sentence: Give the report to *whoever* asks for it.

You cannot always rely on sound to help choose the correct pronoun. See Learning Tip 7 for a superior method of choosing correctly between subjective and objective case.

Learning Tip 3: To determine whether to use *more than me* or *more than I,* complete the thought the comparison expresses.

John is taller than *me.* (*Than me am* is the comparison expressed.)

Therefore, the correct sentence should read

John is taller than *I.* (*than I am*)

Learning Tip 4: A pronoun in an appositive must be in the same case as the word it complements, called the *antecedent.* Mentally replace the noun antecedent with the pronoun from the appositive to determine which case to use.

Example:	The students, Jack and *(she/her),* passed the test.
Replace noun:	*She* passed the test.
Correct version:	The students, Jack and *she,* passed the test.

Students is the subject of the verb *passed;* therefore, the appositive must be in the subjective case.

Example:	The test was passed by the students, Jack and *(she/her).*
Replace noun:	The test was passed by *her.*
Correct version:	The test was passed by the students, Jack and *her.*

Students is the object of the preposition *by;* therefore, the appositive must be in the objective case.

See Learning Tip 10 for similar directives about pronouns used with noun antecedents.

Learning Tip 5: *Myself* is often used incorrectly in place of a subjective-case or an objective-case pronoun, as follows:

NOT:	Another person and *myself* witnessed the accident.
	Both Ms. Watson and *myself* want to participate.
BUT:	Another person and *I* witnessed the accident.
	Both Ms. Watson and *I* want to participate.
NOT:	Ms. Watson invited Mervin and *myself* to the party.
	Please send all inquiries to Ms. Watson or *myself.*
BUT:	Ms. Watson invited Mervin and *me* to the party.
	Please send all inquiries to Ms. Watson or *me.*

Do not use *myself* in a sentence unless the pronoun *I* appears in the same sentence. For example:

> I will schedule the budget meeting myself.
> I will talk to Mr. Jones myself.
> I will finish the project by myself.

2. Use subjective-case pronouns as subject complements following state-of-being verbs.

You should memorize the eight state-of-being verbs: *am, is, are, was, were, be, been, being*.

A *subject complement* is a noun, pronoun, or adjective that follows a state-of-being verb used as a main verb. Subject complements as nouns that follow state-of-being verbs are called *predicate nouns*; pronouns are called *predicate pronouns*; and adjectives are called *predicate adjectives*. Predicate pronouns are always subjective-case pronouns.

> The committee chairman is *he*.
> The presidential candidates are *they*.
> The student who took the exam is *she*.
> The performer is *who*?

> **NOT:**   The programmers are *them* who developed the software.

> **BUT:**   The programmers are *they* who developed the software.

Learning Tip 6: Think of the state-of-being verb as an equal sign (=). Just as you can reverse a mathematical equation around the equal sign without changing the equation's meaning, so you can reverse the parts of a sentence around the state-of-being verb without changing the meaning of the sentence. For example:

> The company director is (=) *she*.

can be reversed to read

> *She* is (=) the company director.

Therefore, when you see a state-of-being verb that is followed by a pronoun, read the pronoun that follows the state-of-being verb first; then, read the state-of-being verb; and, finally, read the part of the sentence that comes before the state-of-being verb.

> The first speaker is (=) *her*.

Her is (=) the first speaker.

If your ear likes the way the reversed sentence order sounds, the pronoun is probably correct. However, relying on sound may not always work and should not substitute for knowing the correct rules. See Learning Tip 7 for an alternative to sound in choosing between subjective and objective case.

The first speaker is (=) *she*.
She is (=) the first speaker.

Learning Tip 7: If you understand thoroughly the two rules for subjective case, you can choose correctly between subjective- and objective-case pronouns in almost every instance. That is, when choosing between subjective- and objective-case pronouns, merely apply the subjective-case rules to your choice. If the pronoun is (1) the subject of a verb or (2) a subject complement, you must use the subjective case. If the pronoun is not the subject of a verb or is not a subject complement, you will almost always choose the objective-case pronoun.

(Who/Whom) did Mr. Garcia say won the election? (The pronoun is the subject of *won*; therefore, subjective-case *who* is correct.)

(Who/Whom) is the person responsible for the delay? (The pronoun is the subject complement following the state-of-being verb *is*; therefore, subjective-case *who* is correct.)

I will give the commendation to (whoever/whomever) you prefer. (The first verb is *will give*; its subject is *I*. The second verb is *prefer*; its subject is *you*. Therefore, the left-over pronoun is neither a subject of a verb nor a subject complement; and the objective-case *whomever* is correct.)

RULES FOR OBJECTIVE CASE

3. Use the objective case to name the receiver of an action (object of the verb).

The director asked *him* for financial advice.
The two women thanked *whom*?
The manager questioned *me* about the report.

Learning Tip 8: **Direct objects** answer the questions *whom?* or *what?* about the subject and its verb. You can easily locate the direct object of the verb by saying the verb and asking *whom?* or *what?* For example, in *The two women thanked him*, say the verb *thanked* and ask *whom?* The answer is *him.* So *him* is the direct object of the verb.

Learning Tip 9: **Indirect objects** precede direct objects and answer the questions *for whom?* or *for what?* or *to whom?* or *to what?* about the subject and its verb.

Give *John* the *book.* (*John* is the indirect object; *book* is the direct object.)

My supervisor called *John* and *me* into his office. (whom)

Millie sold *them* a new station wagon. (to whom)

---

4. Use objective-case pronouns as objects of prepositions.

A preposition is a connective that shows the relationship of a noun or a pronoun to some other word in the sentence. A prepositional phrase consists of a preposition and its object and modifiers and may be used as a noun, an adjective, or an adverb. Some common prepositions and prepositional phrases are the following:

about	*about* him and her	**from**	*from* you and me
above	*above* them	**in**	*in* whom we trust
across	*across* the street from us	**inside**	*inside* us
after	*after* them	**near**	*near* them
against	*against* us	**of**	*of* us
at	*at* us	**on**	*on* them
before	*before* them	**through**	*through* us
beside	*beside* you and me	**to**	*to* you and me
between	*between* you and me	**toward**	*toward* them
by	*by* them	**under**	*under* them
down	*down* by the river	**up**	*up* to us
except	*except* us	**with**	*with* him and her
for	*for* whom the bell tolls	**within**	*within* us

NOT: The sales representative demonstrated the operation of the new equipment to *we* keyboard operators.

BUT: The sales representative demonstrated the operation of the new equipment to *us* keyboard operators. (*Us* keyboard operators is the object of the preposition *to*.)

Learning Tip 10: When a pronoun is used with a noun antecedent, omit the noun to determine whether subjective or objective case is required.

Example:	*(We/Us)* students are prepared for the exam.
Omit noun:	*We* are prepared for the exam.
Correct version:	*We* students are prepared for the exam.

The pronoun *we* complements the noun *students*. Because *students* is the subject of the sentence, the pronoun must be in the subjective case—*we*.

Example:	Melvin was right to go along with *(we/us)* students.
Omit noun:	Melvin was right to go along with *us*.
Correct version:	Melvin was right to go along with *us* students.

Us students is the object of the preposition *with*. Therefore, the pronoun must be in the objective case—*us*.

See Learning Tip 4 for similar directives about pronouns in appositives.

---

5. Use an objective-case pronoun as the subject or object of an infinitive.

An infinitive is the form of the verb commonly introduced by *to* and therefore consists of the word *to* plus a present-tense verb (such as *to run, to jump, to sing*).

| Subject of infinitive: | I want *her* to teach the class. |
| | The president told *her* to prepare the annual report. |

| Object of infinitive: | Do you plan to ask *them* to participate? |
| | I want to designate *her* as an alternate member. |

| **NOT:** | My supervisor called *he* and *I* to meet in his office. |
| | I intend to counsel *you* and *she* against the move. |

| **BUT:** | My supervisor called *him* and *me* to meet in his office. |
| | I intend to counsel *you* and *her* against the move. |

RULES FOR POSSESSIVE CASE

---

6. To form the possessive for a singular or a plural noun, add *'s*. If the noun ends in *s*, add only an apostrophe.

CASE   11

Singular	Plural
child = child's	children = children's
man = man's	men = men's
lady = lady's	ladies = ladies'
Robert = Robert's	Mr. Roberts = Mr. Roberts'
company = company's	companies = companies'
boss = boss'	bosses = bosses'

Learning Tip 11: Some style manuals recommend forming the possessive of a noun ending in *s* by adding *'s* if the extra *s* is sounded. For example:

the boss's letter   St. Louis's business center
the witness's statement   Dallas's Convention Center

This practice is also correct. However, for simplicity and consistency purposes, Rule 6 as stated is recommended and will be reflected in the answers to all exercises in *Practical Grammar Review*.

Learning Tip 12: To avoid mistakes in forming the possessive of a plural noun, first form the plural and then apply Rule 6.

Singular	Plural	Plural Possessive
boy	boys	boys'
woman	women	women's
alumnus	alumni	alumni's
Jones	Joneses	Joneses'

Learning Tip 13: The apostrophe is used to show possession. Do not make an apostrophe error by putting an apostrophe in a plural noun. For example:

NOT: We are having steak's for dinner.
           The Carter's live in the old Zang mansion.

BUT: We are having steaks for dinner.
           The Carters live in the old Zang mansion.

7. To make a pronoun possessive, use the possessive form of the pronoun. Do not add an apostrophe to the pronoun.

The common possessive pronouns are *my, mine, your, yours, his, hers, its, our, ours, their, theirs,* and *whose*. Notice that an apostrophe is not used in any possessive pronoun.

> The report is missing *its* cover sheet.
> The director lost *his* seat on the board.
> Susan asked whether the blue suitcase is *hers*.
> The committee wondered *whose* proposal to consider first.

Learning Tip 14: Two especially troublesome possessive pronouns are *its* and *whose*. Any time you are tempted to put an apostrophe in *it's* or *who's*, remember the apostrophe forms a contraction but not a possessive:

> **it's** = *it is* or *it has* (but never the possessive pronoun *its*)
> **who's** = *who is* or *who has* (but never the possessive pronoun *whose*)

> **NOT:**　　The software documentation is missing *it's* index.
> 　　　　　James is the person *who's* father is in Germany.

> **BUT:**　　The software documentation is missing *its* index.
> 　　　　　James is the person *whose* father is in Germany.

8. To show that two or more words jointly possess the same thing, form the possessive on the last word only. To show separate possession, form the possessive on each word.

> This company is *Smith and Taylor's* law firm. (One firm is owned jointly by Smith and Taylor.)
> *Mother and Dad's* stocks are increasing in value. (The stocks are owned jointly by Mother and Dad.)
> They are *Mr. Reynold's and Mr. Anderson's* attorneys. (Refers to two attorneys.)
> *Chicago's and New York's* police forces are among the most highly trained in undercover work. (Refers to the police force of each city separately.)

Learning Tip 15: If two persons jointly possess the same thing and if a pronoun is used to identify one of the persons, both the noun and the pronoun must show possession.

> *His* and *Grandma's* house is located on State Street.

A gerund is a verb form that ends in *-ing* and functions as a noun. When gerunds occur as phrases, the entire phrase functions as a noun.

A noun or a pronoun that immediately precedes a gerund is usually in the possessive case.

NOT: The *driver speeding* terrified us.
             Margo singing in the choir contributed greatly to the alto section.

BUT: The *driver's speeding* terrified us.
             Margo's singing in the choir contributed greatly to the alto section.

Writers should not confuse gerund phrases with participial phrases that function as adjectives rather than as nouns. For example:

    We saw Luke playing golf.

Playing golf is a participial phrase modifying *Luke*.

Sometimes, a subtle difference in meaning affects the choice between objective or possessive case. For example:

    Luke watched *them* golfing.
    Luke watched *their* golfing.

In the first sentence, the emphasis is on the **performer** of the action of *golfing*. Golfing in this situation is a participle modifying *them*.

In the second sentence, the emphasis is on the **action** of golfing. *Golfing* this time is a gerund, and *their* is a possessive pronoun modifying the gerund. The possessive shows that what concerns the writer is not the person but the action.

Normally, possessive case is not used when the noun preceding a gerund is (1) an abstract noun or (2) a noun followed by a prepositional phrase.

NOT: The situation was one of *dishonesty's* getting the upper hand.
             Mr. Sill did not appreciate the director's *of the department* getting Friday off.

BUT: The situation was one of dishonesty getting the upper hand.
             Mr. Sill did not appreciate the director of the department getting Friday off.

CASE SELF-EVALUATION

Write *C* if the sentence is correct; write *I* if the sentence is incorrect. Compare your answers with those on the answer sheet. For each item you missed, review the explanation and, if necessary, study the material again.

_____ 1. Jack stressed the value of keeping the computer access codes among us managers.

_____ 2. The report on personnel allocation's for next quarter is missing it's table of contents.

_____ 3. The space-allocation directors, Morris and me, were awarded a special commendation for efficiency.

_____ 4. Tom and she are the researchers who completed the analysis for the State Department.

_____ 5. The computer-center director asked Ralph to check out the graphics software to whomever has a validated pass.

_____ 6. The project supervisor asked her to prepare the quarterly progress report.

_____ 7. His quitting affected the effectiveness of the budget committee. [emphasis on action]

_____ 8. Claire's and Nancy's reports are quite different from each other.

_____ 9. The inspector will observe Mr. Morris's performance on Friday afternoon.

_____ 10. Sue approved of him amending the motion to table further study of the project. (emphasis on action)

_____ 11. Bryan assigned he and I the task of interpreting the results of the marketing study.

_____ 12. Mike is a more effective speaker than me.

_____ 13. The first speaker on the conference program will be her.

_____ 14. All the supervisors' offices will be equipped with personal computers.

_____ 15. Whose going to represent us at the Regional Management Symposium?

_____ 16. Mr. Terrazas requested Jerrilyn and myself to head the committee.

_____ 17. She and Mother's plan is to split the work load between he and you.

_____ 18. Us supervisors must work on Labor Day.

CASE

ANSWERS TO CASE SELF-EVALUATION

1.   C   The objective case *us* is used to complete a prepositional phrase. (Rule 4; LT10)

2.   I   Plurality but not possessive case is required in *allocations*. (LT13) Use *its* for the possessive form of *it*. No apostrophe is needed. (Rule 7; LT14)

3.   I   The appositive *Morris and I* has to be in the subjective case because its antecedent, *space-allocation directors*, is the sentence subject. (LT4)

4.   C   Subjective-case *Tom and she* are the subject of *are*. (Rule 1; LT 1) Use *who* because it serves as the subject of the verb *completed*. (Rule 1; LT2; LT7)

5.   I   The pronoun serves as the subject of the verb *has* rather than as the direct object of the preposition *to*, so subjective-case *whoever* is correct. (Rule 1; LT2; LT7)

6.   C   Use objective case *her* as the subject of an infinitive. (Rule 5)

7.   C   The possessive case *his* is used when a pronoun is the subject of a gerund and the emphasis is on the action. (Rule 9)

8.   C   Use singular possession because individually owned reports are referred to. (Rule 8)

9.   I   Use only an apostrophe to show possessive case in a noun that ends in *s*. (LT11)

10. I   Use the possessive case *his* when a pronoun is placed before a gerund and the emphasis is on the action. (Rule 9)

11. I   The compound indirect object must be objective-case *him* and *me*. (Rule 3; LT8)

12. I   Use subjective case after completing the clause with *than I am*. (LT3)

13. I   Use the subjective-case *she* following a state-of-being verb. (Rule 2; LT6; LT7)

14. C   Plural possession in words ending in *s* is shown with an apostrophe. (Rule 6; LT12)

15. I   *Who's* is the contraction for *who is*. *Whose* should not be used. (Rule 7; LT14)

16. I   Direct objects require objective case (*Jerrilyn and me*). (Rule 3; LT8; LT9; LT5)

17. I   *Her and Mother's* is required because a pronoun and a noun possess the same thing. (LT15) Objects of the preposition *between* require objective case. (Rule 4; LT7)

18. I   By mentally deleting *supervisors*, you can determine that *we* must be used. (LT10)

CASE EXERCISE 3

Name_____

Write *A* if the first choice in parentheses is correct; write *B* if the second choice is correct. Some sentences have more than one answer.

_____ 1. My (mother and dad's/mother's and dad's) home was appraised for $182,000.

_____ 2. Erin will cooperate with (whoever/whomever) is in charge of the investigation.

_____ 3. The winner of the public-speaking contest is (she/her).

_____ 4. (Yours/Your's) is the only houseboat with (its/it's) windows intact.

_____ 5. The treasurer requested (he/him) and (she/her) to contact the Payroll Office.

_____ 6. That (manager's/managers') actions seem to be subject to ridicule.

_____ 7. The information given to (we/us) temporary (worker's/workers) is appreciated.

_____ 8. Her current status with the (Citizen's/Citizens') Awareness Committee was reported by (who/whom)?

_____ 9. Dr. Thompson asked (he/him) and (they/them) to help with the research.

_____10. Please give the keys to (whoever/whomever) plans to leave the building last.

_____11. The (women's/womens') clothing will be moved to the third floor.

_____12. Ms. Webber does not know (who's/whose) signature is on the application.

_____13. Larraine heard on the television that the winning entry was (her's/hers).

_____14. Ms. Markham disclosed we are (they/them) (who/whom) were selected for the awards.

_____15. (Pauline/Pauline's) and (Bess'/Bess's) scores improved significantly on Form B.

_____16. Mr. Bradford greatly appreciates (you/your) agreeing to chair the committee. (emphasis on action)

_____17. Ms. Osmond was present, and (Clay/Clay's) discussing the budget surprised her. (emphasis on performer of action)

_____18. (Who/Whom) attended the awards dinner with (he/him)?

_____19. Mrs. Knight wants only (he/him) to deliver her groceries.

CASE   19

CASE EXERCISE 4   Name_____

Underline the subject of each clause once; underline the verb or verb phrase of each clause twice; and enclose each dependent clause in brackets. Then, apply Learning Tip 7 by writing *S* for subjective case and *O* for objective case.

_____ 1. (Who/Whom) did you vote for in last year's election?

_____ 2. With (who/whom) were you consulting during the month of July?

_____ 3. (Who/Whom) shall we say prepared the report?

_____ 4. The question of (who/whom) Ms. Quayle should appoint continues to be an issue.

_____ 5. (Who/Whom) did Mr. Oveson think was selected?

_____ 6. (Who/Whom) could it have been?

_____ 7. The choice of (who/whom) will be selected has not been determined.

_____ 8. (Who/Whom) were you thinking about when you bought the present?

_____ 9. Jake wants to know (who/whom) you think should be elected.

_____ 10. (Whoever/Whomever) you recommend will be placed on the school-board ballot.

_____ 11. Jake will interview (whoever/whomever) meets the company's minimum qualifications.

_____ 12. Jake will talk with (whoever/whomever) you recommend.

_____ 13. Jake will talk with (whoever/whomever) answers the classified ad.

_____ 14. Jake will give the assignment to (whoever/whomever) you think you can recommend.

_____ 15. Jake will give the assignment to (whoever/whomever) you think can be recommended.

_____ 16. Please write immediately to (whoever/whomever) you think can provide the data.

_____ 17. Please vote for the student (who/whom) you think has done the best in Economics 101.

_____ 18. The person (who/whom) I was talking about doesn't have the appropriate background.

_____ 19. Jake is the one (who/whom) we think will attend.

_____ 20. The executive (who/whom) we invited to participate cannot attend.

Write the letter identifying the one best answer.

_____ 1.   a.   Will you be able to go to Lagoon with John and I?
        b.   The principal gave Robert and him the data from the teachers' conference.
        c.   The teacher who must conduct the teaching seminar is me.

_____ 2.   a.   The advisory committee presented a new plan to we employees.
        b.   Between you and I, Joe is uncertain whether he should accept your offer.
        c.   After the meetings are over, please write a report summarizing the outcomes for Doris and me.

_____ 3.   a.   A meeting was scheduled with Douglas' and Howard's teacher to discuss their English grades.
        b.   Mitt Daley's and his father's birthdays occur between Thanksgiving and Christmas.
        c.   The results are contained in Ms. Daines's and Mr. Dant's evaluation.

_____ 4.   a.   Can Dr. Parsons attend the tenure meeting with Dr. Horton and I?
        b.   The security person asked her and me to check all the doors before leaving.
        c.   The accountants requested she and I to meet with them next Friday morning.

_____ 5.   a.   Lieutenant Mierisch asked who is responsible for the change in policy.
        b.   Whom do you think will be willing to accept the responsibility?
        c.   Judge Rosen's memorandum is about who?

_____ 6.   a.   Who did he or she nominate during the budget hearings?
        b.   Ms. Meza is the person who, you will recall, was offered the job a year ago.
        c.   Mr. Mikita is he who we asked to lead the discussion.

_____ 7.   a.   Marla expects that us eating in the classroom will stop at once. (emphasis on action taken)
        b.   I cannot support Orson and Parley substituting as teachers. (emphasis on performer of action)
        c.   Word of Marshall's abandoning the project proved to be false. (emphasis on performer of action)

_____ 8.   a.   The Hawaiians presented a different viewpoint to we mainlanders.
        b.   We purchasing agents demand our share of vacation time.
        c.   The woman who ordered the new venetian blinds is her.

_____ 9.   a.   The workers' expressed interest in having the seminar repeated at an earlier hour.
        b.   Did you attend Dr. Shields lecture on organizational behavior?
        c.   The professor's secretary resigned yesterday because of a salary dispute.

Name_____

Write the letter identifying any correct sentences. Some items may have more than one answer.

_____ 1. a. No one in my department earns as much as her.
           b. The most-proficient workers in my department are you and she.
           c. Were you at the meeting when us accountants gave our analysis of the data?

_____ 2. a. Both you and him should stay out of the sun as much as possible.
           b. Throughout the trip, the dog sat between his master and I.
           c. No one except you and me knows the combination to the safe.

_____ 3. a. Yesterday, I reviewed the salary schedule with both him and his coworkers.
           b. Karla and she are trying to get employment as English teachers in Russia.
           c. Two employees, Margaret and he, will be replaced in about six months.

_____ 4. a. Earl is the computer programmer who Ms. Muse mentioned in her report.
           b. Whomever you select will undoubtedly have the approval of Mr. Morley.
           c. We need a technician who, as you might expect, can service our personal computers.

_____ 5. a. Every one of the referees except he has been assigned to a game in January.
           b. Mr. Laxton is just as good a coordinator as she.
           c. The players would rather choose Molly than me.

_____ 6. a. Who's the recipient of the outstanding employee award—Benjamin or she?
           b. Ellen answered by saying, "It was he who made the decision."
           c. The store, contrary to our expectations, billed my wife and me for the damages.

_____ 7. a. Separate job applications were submitted by Sheldon LeBaron and me.
           b. Mr. Laxton plans to encourage you and she to attend a local junior college.
           c. The engineer told we technicians that she had reached a decision.

_____ 8. a. The refrigerator was on it's side with it's compressor damaged.
           b. I'm sure the apartment will be ours if we are willing to sign a lease
           c. This report of hers is very pointed in its analysis of our budget problems.

_____ 9. a. The men's and women's clothing this year reflects many features of the clothing of the 1960s.
           b. When you send you're order to us, be sure to include a purchase-order number.
           c. We appreciate your order for a six month's supply of safety matches.

_____ 10. a. My mom and dad's home will be for sale in about six months.
           b. His and Mom's house is located in the suburbs of Chicago.
           c. Lauritzen and Lawson's law firm is in the east wing of the University Mall.

Edit to correct all case errors. Two sentences contain no errors.

1.   Sonya is the one who's mother baked the apple pies for Gregg and I.

2.   Dillon is more efficient than me, and I want to become as efficient as him.

3.   Deverl confidently said, "It was he to whom you spoke yesterday."

4.   Valerie is she who plans to pass the assignment along to Annick or myself.

5.   Of all the people who I know, he is the one who I can rely on when I get in a bind.

6.   Between you and I, all the students except she took the examination on time.

7.   Ms. Howe and he asked whether the contract is satisfactory to we homeowners.

8.   The secret agreement between Mr. Kwan and I will raise it's ugly head in July.

9.   Both students, Steve and he, will be our's to use for decorating purposes this weekend.

10.   The sales representative us managers want to send to the meeting is him.

11.   No one but my friend and myself participated; but the winner of the dispute is not he.

12.   Henry designated her as the candidate who he thinks has the best background for the job.

13.   I want to choose Mugdawan and she to be responsible for the after-game dinner's.

14.   The results of that survey of your's will be made available to whomever requests them.

CASE EXERCISE 8   Name_____

Edit to correct all case errors. Two sentences contain no errors.

1. The books that him and Ann used were provided to he and she by myself and Dr. Jones.

2. Our group (Lee, June, and I) gave all group members' ideas to him and her.

3. The main subgroup who's tasks' were so difficult consisted of Bill, Jack, and myself.

4. Although the struggle for power between Jodi and I continued, it's impact's were negligible.

5. If I were him and she were me, the discrimination among we employee's would cease.

6. The meetings at the McGuire's home were attended by everyone except Elaine and I.

7. Suzie said, "If anyone in Keith and Frank's offices' goes to Seattle, it will be her."

8. Whom did you ask to prepare the specifications for us architects at Carlile and Ayers?

9. I was told that we workers are to honor Aprils' discounts for him and her.

10. Carson City and Las Vegas's police forces will respond to Mr. Walker and myself.

11. "Pizza at it's best" is the theme proposed by Ms. Durwood and they.

12. Yes, the one's whom Ned says will get travel clearance might be Tom and I.

13. The childs' bicycles were sold to they who bid the highest at Salt Lake Cities' auctions.

14. You receiving the scholarship was made known to Lorenzo and I when we arrived today.

AGREEMENT AND REFERENCE

AGREEMENT DISCUSSION

Agreement shows the relationship between nouns and pronouns and their verbs and between nouns and their corresponding pronouns. *Agreement* specifies a singular noun or pronoun uses a singular verb, a plural noun or pronoun takes a plural verb, a singular pronoun refers to a singular noun, and a plural pronoun refers to a plural noun.

Your writing will have correct agreement if you

1. locate the true subject of the clause, and
2. make the verb agree with the subject. In addition,
3. locate the noun of the clause in which a pronoun is used, and
4. make the pronoun agree in number with the noun.

Thus:

singular = singular

> she has; object is; he advocates; the child wants
> Joan = she; Danny = he; corporation = it

plural = plural

> they have; animals are; rockets blast; the authors write
> David and Renee = they; children = they

TERMINOLOGY

Antecedent—The noun for which a pronoun substitutes.

> The *students* have spent many hours studying for *their* examinations. (Antecedent of *their* is *students*.)

Collective noun—A noun that names a group or collection of persons or things. When the group is acting in unison, a singular verb is used; but when the group is acting as separate individuals, a plural verb is used.

The *jury* agrees on the verdict. (Singular verb because *jury* is acting in unison.)

The *committee* are at odds on a possible decision. (Plural verb because the *committee* is not acting in unison.)

Compound subject—A subject composed of two or more sentence elements joined with a conjunction.

The *monkeys* and the *lions* are the most-popular attractions in the zoo.
Pleasure and *exercise* are derived from walking to work each day.

Essential (restrictive) clause—A clause that is essential to the meaning of the sentence. Commas are not used to set off essential clauses.

The worker *who proposed the improved plan* was promoted.
The item *that was missing from the envelope* is needed before the tax audit.

Expletive—The words *it* and *there* used in a sentence but having no meanings or antecedents.

It is said the bill will keep government out of our pockets.
There are more assignments in this course than in any of my other courses.

Indefinite pronoun—A pronoun (such as *every*, *nobody*, and *someone*) that classifies a group of persons or things rather than a specific person or thing.

Can't *anybody* relate to my problems?
If *anyone* can attend, we'll be able to use the coupon.

Modifier—An adjective or adverb used to describe a noun, a verb, or an adjective.

The *brown, rusty* desk stands *lonely* in the corner like a *forlorn* creature.
A *really well-kept* yard adds beauty to the *entire* neighborhood.

Nonessential (nonrestrictive) clause—A clause that is not essential to the meaning of the sentence. Nonessential clauses are set off in the sentence, usually with commas.

The Management Club, *which meets in Room 203,* will elect a new president today.
A successful person, *who may also be wise,* can enjoy many benefits from retirement.

Number—The agreement between the subject and its verb and between a noun and its pronoun: A singular subject requires a singular verb; a plural subject requires a plural verb. A singular noun requires a singular pronoun; a plural noun requires a plural pronoun.

His *manner* of speaking *demonstrates* his upbringing.
The *women* in the firm *demonstrate* a willingness to work together.
A successful *manager* always tries to better *his or her* employees.
The *teachers* you seek are in *their* offices.

Parenthetical phrase—A phrase that interrupts a sentence to qualify or explain. Parenthetical phrases are typically surrounded by commas.

The principal amount, *more than we expected*, is due no later than the 10th.
As he stated, *stumbling over his words*, no one has a better wife than does he.

Person—The state of the pronoun indicating (1) the person speaking, (2) the person spoken to, or (3) the person spoken about.

First person: *I, me, mine, we, us, our, ours*
Second person: *you, your, yours*
Third person: *he, him, his, she, her, hers, it, its, they, them, their, theirs, who, whom, whose*

I started slowly this morning when *my* alarm failed to ring. (first)
You will do well to concentrate on *your* studies. (second)
Their party was a great success according to *him* and *her*. (third)

Preposition—A word used in a sentence to show relationships. Common prepositions include *by, between, among, in, for, of, above, with, except,* and *under*.

Ralph noticed a bright red stain *in* the rug.
Linda helped the homeless people living *under* the bridge.
The cookies were baked just *for* you and me.

Prepositional phrase—A group of words consisting of a preposition and its object.

Look *in the overhead compartment for carry-on luggage*.
By the way, **with** the contract **in our hands**, you'll receive a nice bonus.

Reference—Agreement in number, person, and gender between a pronoun and its noun antecedent.

When *a person* makes a bold statement, *he or she* should be prepared to provide the facts.

All *prescription drug companies* are required to submit *their* formulas to the FDA.
Our *director* has indicated *he* plans to take his vacation in August.
Please ring for the *nurse* and ask *her* to come as quickly as possible.

Relative clause—A clause introduced by a relative pronoun such as *who, that,* or *which.*

All people *who were invited* are here.
The exam items *that caused problems* came from Chapter 9.

Relative pronoun—A pronoun such as *who, that,* and *which* that functions as a connective in the dependent clause it introduces and that connects to the rest of the sentence.

Men and women who are qualified should apply for the exemption.
The *letters that* were received today are on the table.
The *apple pie, which* is delicious, is in the refrigerator.

Unit of measurement—Any noun designating a measuring standard—*i.e.*, money, time, fractions, distances, weights, and quantities.

Driving *50 miles* a day is of little concern to committed commuters.
Your allowance has been raised to *$25* a week.
A total of *15 pounds* was my weight gain over the holidays.

RULES FOR AGREEMENT

1.   Use a verb that agrees in number with its subject.

Jean *is applying* for entrance into the accounting program. (singular)
Dennis and Lynn *are processing* their applications for employment. (plural)
The book on manners *has been* on reserve for three months. (singular)
Manners *help create* favorable impressions regardless of the circumstances. (plural)

Learning Tip 1: In a compound or a complex sentence, identify the true subject of a clause before determining the plurality of its verb.

When *sales personnel demonstrate* the machines, *the personnel appear* to know all technical specifications. (Both clauses have plural subjects and use plural verbs.)

When *Tom was dating* Ruth, *he sent* her flowers for every special occasion. (Both clauses contain singular subjects and use singular verbs.)

Database and word processing programs sell better than other software, but the *spreadsheet program* also *sells* well. (Plural = plural in first clause; singular = singular in second clause.)

One of the people *who are* invited *is* the president of the travel agency. (Subject *one* is singular and uses the singular verb *is*. Second subject *who* is plural and takes the plural verb *are*.)

---

2. Use a plural verb when two separate subjects are joined with *and*.

The *time* and the *place* of the meeting *have been* set.

Working in the morning and *boating in the afternoon provide* a sense of satisfaction.

Learning Tip 2: If the two subjects of a compound can be split and used with singular verbs as two separate sentences without changing the basic wording, the sentence has a compound subject and requires a plural verb. Otherwise, if the compound subject refers to the same person or object or represents a single idea, the entire subject is singular and takes a singular verb.

For example, "*Working in the morning and boating in the afternoon provide* a sense of satisfaction" is tested as follows:

> *Working in the morning* provides a sense of satisfaction.
> *Boating in the afternoon* provides a sense of satisfaction.

Thus, *Working in the morning and boating in the afternoon* requires the plural verb *provide*.

However, note "*Research and development is* an integral part of our corporation."

> *Research is* an integral part of our corporation.
> *Development is* an integral part of our corporation.

This change does not pass the test because the meaning of the sentence is changed with *development is*. Thus, *research and development* is considered a singular subject and requires the singular verb *is*.

Learning Tip 3: To avoid confusion, restate the article when the compound subject is plural. In the following example, notice that the singular items represent one person or idea and that the plural items represent two people or ideas:

Singular: My friend and roommate

The secretary and treasurer
Their research and development

Plural: My friend and my roommate
The secretary and the treasurer
Their research and their development

---

3.   **Use a singular verb when two singular subjects are joined with *or* or *nor*. When a singular subject and a plural subject are joined with *or* or *nor*, the verb takes the number of the subject closer to the verb.**

Either Rachael or Eric *is* scheduled next.
Neither money nor power *is* justification for rude manners.
Neither the computer nor the software programs *were delivered* today.
None of the chairs or the table *looks* damaged.

Learning Tip 4: To avoid a sentence that sounds incorrect, such as the fourth example above, restructure the sentence to place the plural subject to the right of the conjunctions *or* and *nor*. In this way, a plural verb will always be used with a plural subject.

Neither the table nor the chairs *look* damaged.
A large auditorium or separate meeting rooms *are* available for your speakers.
Neither a textbook nor papers *are* allowed in the examination room.

Learning Tip 5: In some sentences, particularly those worded as questions, restructure the sentence to locate the subject and verb before applying the rule.

NOT: Is the manager or the sales personnel available?
Was the book or the letters on the table this morning?
Are Christmas or New Year's Day celebrated in your country?

BUT: The manager or the sales personnel *are* available.
The book or the letters were on the table this morning.
Christmas or New Year's Day is celebrated in your country.

Learning Tip 6: Avoid using *and/or* to join compound subjects. Rewording the subject to use the conjunction *and* or the conjunction *or* is preferable in formal writing.

NOT: Either a new car *and/or* a new boat will be acceptable for my graduation present.
You may work on Mondays *and/or* Wednesdays.
Your pay will be given either in cash *and/or* a check.

BUT: Either a new car *or* a new boat *or* both will be acceptable for my graduation present.

You may work on Mondays *or* Wednesdays *or* both Mondays and Wednesdays.

Your pay will be given either in cash *or* a check *or* both.

---

4. Disregard explanatory phrases, parenthetical phrases, or other modifiers that come between the subject and the verb in deciding if a subject is singular or plural.

The attorney's *briefcase*, along with a box of important papers, *is* by the desk.

Jack, along with Joan, *supports* the proposition.

The *report*, with its poor documentation, *indicates* a change is necessary.

---

5. Use singular verbs with indefinite pronouns.

Indefinite pronouns include *anybody, anyone, any one, anything, each, either, every, everybody, everyone, every one, everything, neither, nobody, no one, nothing, one, somebody, someone,* and *something.* Notice the incorrect and correct uses of these words and their verbs:

NOT: *Everyone* on the committee *plan* to attend the convention.

Neither of us *want* to see the day end.

One thing we all want to do on our vacations this summer *are* to surf in the ocean.

BUT: *Everyone* on the committee *plans* to attend the convention.

Neither of us *wants* to see the day end.

One thing we all want to do on our vacations this summer *is* to surf in the ocean.

Learning Tip 7: Any one and *every one* are written as two words rather than as one when the emphasis is on *one* rather than on *any* or *every.* Also, when an *of* prepositional phrase follows *anyone* or *everyone,* the pronoun is written as two words. Note their correct use in the following sentences:

Anyone is eligible to apply for next year's senior scholarship. (Emphasis is on *any.*)

I have one ticket left. Does *any one* of you want to go. (Emphasis is on *one*; an *of* prepositional phrase follows.)

Everyone is planning to sleep well at the slumber party. (Emphasis is on *every.*)

Every one of the workers is qualified. (Emphasis is on *one*; an *of* prepositional phrase follows.)

Learning Tip 8: The word *none* can be either singular or plural depending on the context of the sentence. When *none* is used as a singular pronoun, it typically means *no one* or *not one*.

SINGULAR: *None* of the workers *has* yet *submitted* a time card.
PLURAL: *None are* so valiant as those who gave *their* lives for their country.

---

6. In a relative clause, use a verb that agrees in number with the antecedent of the relative pronoun.

The words *who, that,* and *which* possessing an antecedent are relative pronouns. For example:

The person *who* succeeds is committed to establishing goals. (The antecedent of the relative pronoun *who* is *person*, requiring the singular verb *is*.)

The letters *that* are on the desk arrived today. (The antecedent of the relative pronoun *that* is *letters*, requiring the plural verb *are*.)

The new rule, *which* takes effect Tuesday, may stifle competition. (The antecedent of the relative pronoun *which* is *rule*, requiring the singular verb *takes*.)

If the antecedent of the relative pronoun is singular, the relative pronoun takes a singular verb. If the antecedent of the relative pronoun is plural, the verb must be plural. For example:

The *person who succeeds* is committed to establishing goals. (*Person* is singular; thus, *who* is singular.)

The *letters that are* on the desk arrived today. (*Letters* is plural; thus, *that* is plural.)

The new *rule, which takes* effect Tuesday, may stifle competition. (*Rule* is singular; thus, *which* is singular.)

Learning Tip 9: Locate the subject and verb of the main clause before determining the verb of the relative pronoun. This practice is particularly helpful in clauses beginning with *one of the* or *one of those* in which the main clause and the relative clause often differ in number.

One of the men who are available is John Truman. (Subject and verb of main clause are *one is*. Subject and verb of relative clause are *who are*.)

One of the qualifying traits that are listed on the form is her strongest attribute. (Subject and verb of main clause are *one is*. Subject and verb of relative clause are *that are*.)

One of the people who are going to the state fair needs to drive. (Subject and verb or main clause are *one needs*. Subject and verb of relative clause are *who are going*.)

---

7. Determine the plurality of collective nouns by using the sense of the sentence. Use a singular verb when members of the group act together or are considered as a unit. Use a plural verb when members act individually or are considered as individual members.

Typical collective nouns are *association, audience, board, class, committee, council, couple, crowd, department, family, firm, group, jury, majority, management, minority, number, pair, press, public, staff, team, tribe,* and *United States*. If you wish to be certain these nouns are plural, use *members of* before the collective noun. Notice their use as singular and plural collectives in the following examples:

SINGULAR (acting as a group):

The *city council* unanimously *agrees* on the decision.
The *firm wants* to delay the environmental impact implementation.
The *United States is* a nation under a democracy.

PLURAL (acting individually):

Management are at odds on the report's projections.
The *family are* unable to reach a decision on this year's vacation plans.
The *jury were* divided on the verdict.

Learning Tip 10: Some style manuals suggest that company and organization names qualify as collective nouns and therefore may be either singular or plural. In addition, a company name is sometimes considered plural if the name ends in an *s* sound. For example:

Markham and Jones *need* your assistance. *They are* looking for additional office space.

Adams and Associates *are* aware of the implications. *They are* making contingency plans for next year.

The Utah Jazz *are* going to qualify for the playoffs. *They* will have the home-court advantage for the first game.

However, in *Practical Grammar Review*, all company and organization names are treated **consistently** as singular nouns. Such consistent treatment eliminates debate about whether some company or organization names should be singular or plural. Therefore:

Markham and Jones *needs* your assistance. *It is* looking for additional office space.

Adams and Associates *is* aware of the implications. *It is* making contingency plans for next year.

The Utah Jazz *is* going to qualify for the playoffs. *It* will have the home-court advantage for the first game.

Learning Tip 11: Like the word *none*, the short words *all, any, more, most,* and *some* are governed by the rule for collectives and are singular or plural according to the intended meaning of the sentence. If a prepositional phrase follows the word, the number of the noun in the phrase controls the number of the verb. If no such phrase follows, the writer signals the intended meaning by his or her choice of the singular or plural verb. For example:

Some of the project has been completed.
Some of the outcomes have been determined.

Most of the report is routine.
Most of the reports are finished.

Which is to be included? (Which one?)
Which are to be included? (Which ones?)

---

8. Use a singular verb in units of measurement when the unit indicates the sum of the whole; use a plural verb when the term emphasizes individual parts.

In determining if a unit of measurement takes a singular or a plural verb, ask yourself if this measurement is one item or a collection of individual items. For example, *$50* is one item and takes a singular verb, but *50 silver dollars* are 50 separate items and take a plural verb. Notice how units of measurement are correctly used as singular and plural forms in the following examples:

SINGULAR:

To a person of 14 contemplating driving, two years *seems* an eternity.
Twenty-six miles *is* the distance covered in the marathon.
Five dollars *is* the price of admission to the museum.

PLURAL:

Two years *are* an eternity to a ten year old.
Twenty-four miles *are* yet to be covered in this 30-mile race.
Ten dollar bills *were* placed in the child's hand.

REFERENCE DISCUSSION

Just as agreement in number is necessary between a subject and its verb, so is agreement between a noun and its pronoun vital to effective communication.

This agreement between a noun and its pronoun as it concerns number, person, and gender is called *reference*. Technically, the noun serving as the antecedent is called the *referent*; however, since it serves the same purpose as an antecedent, it will be called the *antecedent* in this discussion.

When working with pronouns and their antecedents, be certain each pronoun

1.   refers clearly to one specific noun in the same sentence or in a preceding sentence.

2.   agrees with its antecedent in terms of number, person, and gender.

For example, these principles are violated in the following sentences:

NOT: Joan told Lisa *she* would be unable to keep *her* job.
Personnel and management have reached tentative agreement on *its* contract.
Each student is encouraged to submit *their* work on time.

Notice how communication is enhanced when the two principles are correctly applied:

BUT: Joan told Lisa that *Joan* would be unable to keep *her* job.
Personnel and management have reached tentative agreement on *personnel's* contract.
Each student is encouraged to submit *his or her* work on time.

Likewise, reference is unclear when the antecedent does not agree in number, person, or gender with the pronoun:

NOT:	The company gave *their* approval to the vacation plan.
	Each student in the class will submit *their* papers on time.
	Everyone in the group needs *their* picture taken before Monday.

BUT:	The company gave *its* approval to the vacation plan.
	Each student in the class will submit *his or her* papers on time.
	Everyone in the group needs *her or his* picture taken before Monday.

Although the use of *his and her* are correct in working with gender, several procedures are better—such as making nouns plural or establishing the gender of the subject within the sentence. In the examples in *Practical Grammar Review*, however, *his and her* will be used as being correct.

RULES FOR REFERENCE

> **9. Use a pronoun that agrees with its antecedent (referent) in number, in person, and in gender.**

Once a noun is used in a singular or a plural form, use the same form throughout the sentence.

Notice how this rule is applied in the following examples:

Parents give *their* approval when *they* praise *their* children. (Plural noun = plural pronoun.)

Manuel wants a new bicycle added to *his* Christmas list. (Singular noun = singular pronoun.)

Both *boys and girls* are rewarded for *their* insights. (Plural noun = plural pronoun.)

Either a *woman or a man* will be selected depending on *her or his* qualifications. (Singular noun = singular pronoun.)

Learning Tip 12: The rule for collective nouns also applies to noun-pronoun reference. When a group is acting as a unit, the singular pronoun is used. When a group is acting as individuals, the plural pronoun is used.

SINGULAR (acting as a group):

The *County Commission* has announced *its* decision.

The *majority* believe *its* rights have been trampled.
The *public* insists *it's* a victim of the media-ratings game.

PLURAL (acting individually):

Several of the *staff* have said *they* won't approve the proposal.
The *couple* voted differently on issues affecting *their* livelihood.
The *team* are unable to agree on *their* team leader.

---

10. Make the reference obvious when the pronoun can refer to more than one antecedent.

When two or more nouns precede the pronoun, be certain the reader understands to which noun the pronoun refers. Notice the problems in the following sentences and their corrections in the second set of sentences:

NOT: The supervisor told James he would take his vacation in July.
The teacher and the assistant used her bulletin-board ideas.
When you finish reading the body of the report, give it to me.

BUT: The supervisor told James that James would take his vacation in July.
or As the supervisor explained, James will take his vacation in July.
Both the teacher and her assistant used the teacher's bulletin-board ideas.
When you finish reading the body of the report, give the report to me.

Learning Tip 13: To avoid ambiguity and confusion, position the pronoun as closely as possible to its antecedent. (See Modifiers Rule 1.) Avoid the confusion that results in the following sentences:

NOT: The invoice is in the tray that we received in today's mail.
Youth can get a job who have computer skills.

BUT: The invoice that we received in today's mail is in the tray.
Youth who have computer skills can get a job.

---

11. Place the specific-word antecedent of a pronoun in the sentence; do not merely imply the antecedent.

Too often, the pronouns *it, which, this,* and *that* distort meaning when used carelessly. These pronouns may refer to an idea expressed in a preceding part of the sentence if the idea and the reference are unmistakable. Too often, however, an idea clear to the writer is confusing to the reader.

NOT: Although submitted on time, it was totally unorganized.
Missy said she had studied diligently, but no results occurred.
The governor indicated an executive order was coming. This will increase the committee's power.

BUT: Although Kevin submitted his report on time, it was totally unorganized.
Missy said she had studied diligently, but her test results did not show her work.
The Governor indicated an executive order was coming. This order will increase the committee's power.

Learning Tip 14: Unless the meaning is unmistakably clear, the word *this* should always be followed by a noun or a noun phrase. Notice the application of this learning tip in the third sentence above as well as in the following examples:

NOT: No results were forthcoming. This will result in increased costs to taxpayers.
We have the details. This will give impetus to our discussions.

BUT: No results were forthcoming. This lack of results will result in increased costs to taxpayers.
We have the details. This knowledge will give impetus to our discussions.

---

12.   Use the proper relative pronoun to refer to people as well as to introduce essential and nonessential clauses.

The relative pronouns *who, that,* and *which* should be used correctly when they introduce relative clauses:

1.   Use *who, whom,* and *whose* to refer to humans in introducing either essential or nonessential clauses. (*Whose* can also be used to refer to things other than human.)

2.   Use *that* to refer to things other than humans in *essential* clauses.

3.   Use *which* to refer to things other than humans in *nonessential* clauses.

Because *that* and *which* also introduce dependent clauses, the above rules apply to their use as relative pronouns in which an antecedent is stated.

Notice how the relative pronouns are correctly used in the following sentences:

The person *who* will qualify is the one *who* is willing to put forth effort.
The pay period *that* will reflect your raise begins the first of the month.
One method of determining a nonessential clause, *which* is not necessary to the meaning, is to see if the sentence is complete without the clause.

Learning Tip 15: *Essential* clauses do not have commas either before or after them. *Nonessential* clauses are set off with a comma before and a comma after unless the clause comes at the end of a sentence. As a result, *which* clauses should be set off with commas; *that* clauses should not contain commas. Generally, the writer signals the intended meaning to the reader.

Learning Tip 16: Avoid the overuse of the word *that*. In a sentence, *that* has three legitimate uses:

1. as a relative pronoun with a verb and an antecedent,
2. as the first word of a *that* clause, and
3. as a qualifier indicating the one designated noun.

Otherwise, read the sentence omitting the word *that*. If the sentence conveys the same meaning, delete *that* because this extra word dilutes the emphasis of the sentence. Notice the following examples in which *that* is needlessly used:

NOT: The automobile *that* we purchased last month already has engine problems.
The company reported *that* earnings are up 6 percent over last year.
She said *that* he was unfaithful in abiding by the rules of the contract.

BUT: The automobile we purchased last month already has engine problems.
The company reported earnings are up 6 percent over last year.
She said he was unfaithful in abiding by the rules of the contract.

13.   Avoid the expletives *it* and *there* in sentence constructions.

Expletives appear as pronouns but do not function as pronouns because they have no meaning and no antecedents. Although perfectly acceptable in oral speech because voice inflections and oral emphasis convey meaning, expletives should be avoided in writing. They dilute the emphasis of the sentence by moving the most-important part of the sentence to the middle.

NOT: It is said the report's recommendations are well founded.
There are more than 20 million drug users in this country.

It is nice to have you with us today.

BUT: The report's recommendations are well founded.
This country has more than 20 million drug users.
You are welcome to our group today.

As in the above examples, some change of sentence structure is often necessary when the expletive is deleted. This change, however, improves the sentence because the emphasis occurs at one of two points of emphasis—the beginning or the ending of the sentence.

Although expletives are not grammatically incorrect, they reflect second-choice usage in written communication.

Avoid confusing the expletives *it* and *there* with legitimate pronouns. In correct written usage, *it* and *there* will have an antecedent and will have a subject.

AGREEMENT AND REFERENCE SELF-EVALUATION

Write *C* if the sentence is correct; write *I* if the sentence is incorrect. Compare your answers with those on the following page. For each item you missed, review the explanation; if necessary, study the material again.

_____ 1. Five years are a long time to go without realizing a profit.

_____ 2. The book, that I was missing, has been placed in Lost and Found.

_____ 3. My computer displays graphics much faster than yours does.

_____ 4. Neither the teacher nor her students is able to attend the state fair.

_____ 5. One of the women who are available for temporary employment is my sister.

_____ 6. The auditorium can seat 3,000 people that is on the south side of the building.

_____ 7. With the deadline approaching, every one rushed to enroll in the seminar.

_____ 8. A new secretary and a new treasurer are to be elected at Friday's meeting.

_____ 9. Nobody is qualified; therefore, we will reopen our search.

_____ 10. There were approximately 50,000 fans attending the baseball game.

_____ 11. In today's economy, he can get a job if he applies his abilities.

_____ 12. Joan, as well as John, have indicated they will be at the meeting.

_____ 13. The executive vice president told Kent he will leave for Dallas tomorrow.

_____ 14. The press have demanded the right to know all facts pertaining to the issue.

_____ 15. Each student in this class must submit their papers on time.

_____ 16. A desire to learn and a knowledge of the subject contribute to excellent results.

_____ 17. Management must give their approval before the contract is valid.

_____ 18. Winslow and Associates is having an open house on April 1.

_____ 19. Neither of the managers are planning to attend the conference.

ANSWERS TO AGREEMENT AND REFERENCE SELF-EVALUATION

1. I   A singular verb is used with time represented as a unit. (Rule 8)

2. I   The *that* clause is essential to the meaning of the sentence and should not be surrounded by commas. (Rule 12)

3. C   Singular noun *computer* takes the singular verb *displays*. (Rule 1)

4. I   The verb should agree in number with the noun to the right of *or/nor*. (Rule 3)

5. C   The relative pronoun *who* takes the number of its antecedent—*women*. (Rule 6)

6. I   The relative clause should be placed as closely as possible to the pronoun's antecedent, *auditorium*. (Rule 10; LT13)

7. I   Emphasis is on *every*; thus, *everyone* should be one word. (Rule 5; LT7)

8. C   Compound nouns require a plural verb. (Rule 2; LT3)

9. C   Singular verbs are used with indefinite pronouns. (Rule 5)

10. I   The expletive *there* should be avoided. (Rule 13)

11. I   The antecedent of the pronoun *he* should be stated, not implied, to avoid confusion. (Rule 11)

12. I   Explanatory words should be disregarded when you determine the number of a subject and its verb. Thus, the verb and pronoun reference should be singular. (Rule 4)

13. I   The antecedent of the pronoun *he* should be obvious. (Rule 10)

14. I   Collective noun *press* is acting as a group, requiring the singular verb *has*. (Rule 7)

15. I   Singular *each student* requires singular pronouns *his or her*. (Rule 9)

16. C   Compound noun requires the plural verb. (Rule 2)

17. I   Singular collective noun *management* requires singular pronoun *its*. (Rule 9; LT12)

18. C   All company names are treated consistently as singular nouns in *Practical Grammar Review*. (LT10)

19. I   As an indefinite pronoun, *neither* is singular. (Rule 5)

AGREEMENT & REFERENCE EX. 1 Name_____

Write *T* if the statement is true; write *F* if the statement is false.

____ 1.   A compound noun joined by *and* requires a plural verb.

____ 2.   *None* may be used as either a singular or a plural pronoun.

____ 3.   Names of companies as subjects generally require a singular verb.

____ 4.   If a singular noun ends in *s*, a plural verb is used.

____ 5.   Indefinite pronouns, such as *anybody, each,* and *somebody*, require a singular verb.

____ 6.   A plural verb should be used with a collective noun acting as a group.

____ 7.   In a complex sentence, identify the true subject of a clause before determining the number of the verb.

____ 8.   To avoid sound confusion in an *or/nor* clause that contains a singular and a plural noun, place the plural noun to the right of the conjunction.

____ 9.   Reference is defined as agreement in number of the noun and its verb.

____10.   If the reader understands the meaning of the original noun, the pronoun may be used without first indicating the antecedent.

____11.   *Who* should refer to humans, but *that* can refer to either humans or nonhumans.

____12.   The words *all, any, most,* and *some* are governed by the rule for collectives and may be either singular or plural depending on the sense of the sentence.

____13.   A relative pronoun takes the number of its antecedent.

____14.   No confusion results in writing *my friend and roommate* because this reference is obviously to two people and requires a plural verb.

____15.   An approved practice in formal writing is writing *and/or* as a conjunction.

____16.   If the reference appears to be clear, the pronoun *this* may be used without a noun.

____17.   If a prepositional phrase beginning with *of* follows *any one* and *every one*, they are written as two words.

Write *C* to indicate the sentence is correct; write *I* to indicate the sentence is incorrect. Underline the subject of each clause once; underline the verb or verb phrase of each clause twice; and then bracket each dependent clause.

_____ 1. One of the many benefits which are enjoyed by full-time employees is a 10 percent discount on all purchases.

_____ 2. Either the president or the vice president are expected to be in attendance.

_____ 3. The financial statements that supports the new acquisitions are included in your portfolio.

_____ 4. Because math has been a prerequisite for accounting, students possess a better basic understanding than they previously did.

_____ 5. Everything are in readiness for the committee's inspection.

_____ 6. A child needs moral support whenever they try new skills.

_____ 7. Ms. Freeman, not Mr. Jones, needs the report by 8 a.m. tomorrow.

_____ 8. The jury has been unable to reach a decision, resulting in a hung jury.

_____ 9. An analysis of her qualifications proves her the best candidate for the position.

_____10. Shaka said he was concerned because it couldn't be submitted on time.

_____11. Most of the reports has been placed on the manager's desk.

_____12. I have no doubt about it—10 miles are longer than 10 kilometers.

_____13. Walking or jogging in the morning and swimming in the evening help keep your blood pressure normal.

_____14. One of the reports that are on my desk is from the western region.

_____15. The report that I submitted to you contains an error on page 15.

_____16. None is more worthy than those who sacrifice his or her time and abilities.

_____17. You have your choice—you may complete Exercise 7 and/or Exercise 8 on page 254.

_____18. After you have read the report's recommendation, please return it to me.

AGREEMENT AND REFERENCE

Write *A* if the first choice in parentheses is correct; write *B* if the second choice is correct. Some sentences have more than one answer.

_____ 1. Neither Eric nor Wilma (was/were) in class today.

_____ 2. Either (a textbook or paper supplies/paper supplies or a textbook) remain to be purchased for the class.

_____ 3. People who (agree/agrees) with me deserve a special medal.

_____ 4. Children with no parents at home after school should report (his or her/their) status to the main office.

_____ 5. Anyone (who/that) has logged more than 40 hours this week can leave early this evening.

_____ 6. The essay (that/,which) was submitted on time (no punctuation/,) details the life of Andrew Carnegie.

_____ 7. The secretary and treasurer (reports/report) we overspent (its/their) budget.

_____ 8. a. It is a nice day today with temperatures reaching 80 degrees.
         b. Today is nice and warm with temperatures reaching 80 degrees.

_____ 9. None of the group (is/are) able to attend today's session.

_____ 10. One of the items in the parcels (is/are) for Joan Sigart.

_____ 11. The public (has/have) the right to be kept informed by (its/their) elected officials.

_____ 12. a. The group decided it had the right to protest the action.
          b. It decided it had the right to protest the action.

_____ 13. a. Positions can be deleted from a resume that have no bearing on the desired job.
          b. Positions that have no bearing on the desired job can be deleted from a resume.

_____ 14. Trying harder and working more diligently (helps/help) a person achieve success.

_____ 15. (Is/Are) either the sales manager or the sales personnel available at this time?

_____ 16. Management (is/are) trying hard to keep the workers happy.

_____ 17. Willoughby, Miller, and Myers, Inc. (is/are) relocating in the downtown area.

A singular verb or pronoun appears in parentheses in each sentence. On the blank line, write *S* if the verb or pronoun should remain singular; write *P* if the verb or pronoun should be changed to plural. Notice some items have more than one answer.

_____ 1. Which of my past positions (is) to be listed on my resume?

_____ 2. Seeing me in my new dress, which (is) bright green, Julie shrieked with delight.

_____ 3. The department chair and the personnel manager (is) ready for the meeting.

_____ 4. One of the books that (is) required for this course (is) by Ernest Hemingway.

_____ 5. Either problem 1 or problem 2 (is) due tomorrow.

_____ 6. Everyone (talks) about the problem, but no one (does) anything about it.

_____ 7. The Denver Broncos (plans) to play in the Super Bowl in January.

_____ 8. If the answer (appears) true, it likely is correct.

_____ 9. The growth and development of the company (appears) to be a major factor in (its) continuing profit.

_____10. The manager, rather than the workers, (determines) all job-performance standards.

_____11. Reading to blind people and mowing widows' lawns (provides) service to the community.

_____12. No one (has) said anything concerning last night's accident.

_____13. Five dollar bills (was) placed one by one in my hand as a symbol of a debt grudgingly paid.

_____14. After the papers (is) submitted, each (is) to be carefully reviewed.

_____15. I'll check to see if either the table or the chairs (remains) in the room overnight.

_____16. The committee (wants) the director to resign his position.

_____17. Management (desires) to have (its) policies implemented immediately.

_____18. Wilson, Olson, and Christenson, Inc. (expects) that during the winter months (it) will resolve the air-pollution controversy.

Edit the following sentences to correct all agreement and reference errors. Two of the sentences are correct.

1. Take the pan off the stove and put it in the cupboard.

2. We have just one seat left for this performance; does anyone of you want the ticket?

3. A winning smile and a hearty appetite makes a good impression at Mom's Diner.

4. Senator O'Brien has introduced a new bill. This will strengthen the president's powers.

5. The tweed coat, which is on sale, is on display inside the front door.

6. My partner and friend is now available to meet the press.

7. Father and Mother, that were born in Denmark, have recently opened a Danish bakery.

8. My cousin Violet, along with several others, have applied for the secretarial position.

9. It was explained the accident was caused by carelessness.

10. An account of Timm's murder and a story about famine in Africa appears on the front page.

11. We were informed Trace and Company are going public early next year.

12. Bradley appear to be calm prior to his hearing.

13. One of the students who is on the honor roll are going to be my assistant.

14. The team are traveling by bus to Taos; this will help the morale problems.

Edit the following sentences to correct all agreement and reference errors. One sentence is correct.

1. Although the Governor signed the gasoline tax bill, that didn't provide the necessary funds.

2. The San Francisco 49ers are currently leading the league in pass-receiving yards.

3. Because none of the shipments have been received, Ms. Travis have indicated she'll be in touch with all suppliers.

4. Since Eric and Jennifer has been engaged, he or she agrees they need quality time together.

5. Everyone have said they support the president on his health-care reform program.

6. Return the disk to its holder and bring it with you.

7. Before the committee meet this morning, place all papers in its folders.

8. Walking before breakfast and doing pushups after dinner constitute his exercise program.

9. Do anyone here really know what the president believe?

10. The letters are on the table that was received in today's mail.

11. One of the women that is on the jury need disabled assistance.

12. Fifteen dollars are required before anybody enters the road race.

13. Mr. Meeks, the newly appointed chair, and Mr. Hartt, the former chair, has been asked to serve.

TENSE

DISCUSSION

The verb is the most-important word in a sentence. Through the action described by the verb, the sentence comes alive to the reader. As a result, the verb is indeed the lifeblood of the sentence.

Among other properties, verbs tell time by specifying when the action occurred. This time feature is known as *tense*. If the action is currently happening, the verb is in *present tense*. If the action occurred in the past, the verb is in *past tense*. An event yet to happen constitutes *future tense*. The three tenses are illustrated in the following sentences:

> Today, I *examine* the report. (present tense)
> Yesterday, I *examined* the report. (past tense)
> Next Tuesday, I again *will examine* the report. (future tense)

The verb *examine* and its *-ed* derivative indicate the time of the action. Thus, *examine* is *present tense* and *examined* is *past tense*. *Future tense* of a verb is formed by adding *shall* or *will* to the verb.

Some verbs are considered *irregular* because their past tenses do not add a *-d* or an *-ed* suffix to the present tense. However, the principle for using these verbs in present, past, and future tense does not vary, as illustrated:

> Today, I *choose* to attend the meeting. (present tense)
> Yesterday, I *chose* to attend the meeting. (past tense)
> Next week, I again *will choose* to attend the meeting. (future tense)

In the present, past, and future tenses, each described event is a *one-time event*; that is, the sentence *does not* describe an event occurring over a period of time.

When the action occurs over a period of time rather than as one isolated event or when one event precedes another in the past, the tense assumes a *perfect* state. Thus, we have *past perfect, present perfect*, and *future perfect*.

Past perfect indicates an action that was completed before another past action.

I *had finished* the agenda for the meeting before the president asked for it.

Present perfect indicates action started in the past and continuing into the present or action started in the past and completed in the present.

To the present time, I *have attended* many executive meetings.
As of today, I *have completed* all my assignments.

Future perfect shows action yet to begin in the future that will conclude by some specified time.

Prior to the end of the year, I *will have attended* many meetings.

Thus, the primary distinguishing feature between the simple tenses (*present, past*, and *future*) and the perfect tenses (*present perfect, past perfect*, and *future perfect*) is the answer to this question: Is the verb describing one isolated event that is happening, has happened, or will happen (simple tense); or is the verb describing a continuing or a completed (perfected) event (perfect tenses)?

TERMINOLOGY

Future perfect tense—The form of the verb that, in relation to time, shows an action, state of being, or condition that will be completed by or before a specified time in the future. Future perfect tense is formed by adding *shall have* or *will have* to the past participle.

I *will have been employed* here 30 years in May.

Future tense—The form of the verb that, in relation to time, shows an action, state of being, or condition that is associated with the future and that will occur in the future. Future tense is formed by adding *shall* or *will* to the present-tense form of the verb.

Tomorrow I *will speak* to the supervisor about our morale problem.

Conjugation—The result of the inflected forms of a verb that indicate person, number, tense, mood, and voice. To conjugate a verb, arrange the verb forms according to person, tense, or number, as shown in the following table in which the verb *give* is conjugated. Progressive forms may also be conjugated as shown under the definition for *progressive tense* in this section. The following table illustrates the verb in the simple and perfect states as well as the plural and singular forms of the verb in past, present, and future tenses.

Simple Tenses		Perfect Tenses	
Singular	**Plural**	**Singular**	**Plural**
Past			
I gave You gave He, she, it gave	We gave You gave They gave	I had given You had given He, she, it had given	We had given You had given They had given
Present			
I give You give He, she, it gives	We give You give They give	I have given You have given He, she, it has given	We have given You have given They have given
Future			
I will give You will give He, she, it will give	We will give You will give They will give	I will have given You will have given He, she, it will have given	We will have given You will have given They will have given

Gerund—The verb form (verbal) used as a noun and ending in *-ing*. To function as a noun, gerunds may be used as either the subject or the complement in the sentence. For example:

> *Praising the boss* requires stretching the truth. (subject)
> She is *listening* to both sides of the story. (complement)

Historical present—The use of the present tense to make more vivid the description of some past action through a restatement or summarization of the facts from a book, report, letter, etc.

> In his letter, Mr. Williams *states* that he will retire in one year.
> Jesus *says*, "Ask, and it shall be given you."

Infinitive—The verb form (verbal) consisting almost always of *to* plus a verb form. An infinitive may be used as a noun, an adjective, or an adverb. An infinitive is the simple, unconjugated verb, expressing existence or action without reference to person, number, or tense. An infinitive may be used as a subject, complement, or modifier. For example:

> *To have* your input is extremely vital right now. (subject)
> I plan *to visit* my in-laws on our next trip. (complement)
> *To object* to the proposition, he raised his hand and demanded attention. (modifier)

Intransitive verb—A verb that does not need or have an object to complete its meaning. Linking verbs connecting the subject with its complement are always intransitive.

The tennis ball *was returned* before it hit the back line.

Picking up the ringing telephone, she *demanded*, "Who is this?"

Last night I *slept* very well.

Irregular verb—A verb that does not form its past tense and past participle by the addition of *-d* or *-ed*. The following table illustrates the commonly used irregular verb forms.

Present	Past	Past Participle	Present	Past	Past Participle
am	was	been	grow	grew	grown
arise	arose	arisen	hang	hung	hung
bear	bore	borne	have	had	had
bend	bent	bent	hear	heard	heard
bite	bit	bitten	hide	hid	hidden
bid	bid	bid	hit	hit	hit
blow	blew	blown	hold	held	held
break	broke	broken	keep	kept	kept
bring	brought	brought	know	knew	known
build	built	built	lay	laid	laid
buy	bought	bought	lead	led	led
cast	cast	cast	leave	left	left
catch	caught	caught	lend	lent	lent
choose	chose	chosen	let	let	let
come	came	come	lie	lay	lain
cost	cost	cost	lose	lost	lost
deal	dealt	dealt	make	made	made
dig	dug	dug	mean	meant	meant
do	did	done	meet	met	met
draw	drew	drawn	pay	paid	paid
drink	drank	drunk	prove	proved	proven
drive	drove	driven	put	put	put
eat	ate	eaten	quit	quit	quit
fall	fell	fallen	read	read	read
feed	fed	fed	ride	rode	ridden
feel	felt	felt	ring	rang	rung
find	found	found	rise	rose	risen
fling	flung	flung	run	ran	run
fly	flew	flown	say	said	said
freeze	froze	frozen	see	saw	seen
get	got	got	seek	sought	sought
give	gave	given	sell	sold	sold
go	went	gone	send	sent	sent

Present	Past	Past Participle	Present	Past	Past Participle
set	set	set	steal	stole	stolen
sew	sewed	sewn	stick	stuck	stuck
shake	shook	shaken	strike	struck	struck
shine	shone	shone	swear	swore	sworn
show	showed	shown	sweep	swept	swept
shrink	shrank	shrunk	swim	swam	swum
shut	shut	shut	swing	swung	swung
sing	sang	sung	take	took	taken
sink	sank	sunk	teach	taught	taught
sit	sat	sat	tear	tore	torn
sleep	slept	slept	tell	told	told
slide	slid	slid	think	thought	thought
speak	spoke	spoken	throw	threw	thrown
spend	spent	spent	wear	wore	worn
split	split	split	weep	wept	wept
spread	spread	spread	win	won	won
spring	sprang	sprung	wind	wound	wound
stand	stood	stood	write	wrote	written

Participle—A verb form usually ending in *-ing* or *-ed*. A participle may be combined with helping verbs to form verb phrases with different tenses. When a participle is a word standing alone, it is a verbal and functions as a modifier.

The contract, *covering* all details we specified, needs to be signed by both parties.
The woman *standing* next to the desk is a distant relative of mine.
Having specified his major points, the keynote speaker moved to her conclusion.

Past participle—A verb form that ends in *-d* or *-ed* in the case of regular verbs or that is irregularly formed in the case of irregular forms.

She *had analyzed* the report before entering the board room.
The office manager *has shown* the new assistant the office layout.

Past perfect tense—The form of the verb that indicates some action started and completed before some other past action. Past perfect uses the past participle and the helping verb *had*.

In our past relationship, all orders *had been received* before our stipulated deadline.

I *had driven* for many hours before I saw a sign welcoming me to Indiana.

I *had returned* many items of merchandise before I was asked to join the quality-control team.

Past tense—The form of the verb that, in relation to time, shows an action, state of being, or condition associated with the past.

>Mr. Stevens *spoke* at the executive lecture series yesterday.
>I *was asked* to remain after school because I *talked* in class.
>We *delivered* the order this morning.

Present Participle—A verb form that ends in *-ing*. The present participle is formed when *-ing* is added to the present-tense verb. The present participle forms the progressive tense.

>Jacquelyn *is spending* as much time as possible with her grandfather. (present)
>Frank *was complimenting* everyone in the room, hoping for a promotion. (past)
>We *will be hoping* for a change in our income with our next mailing. (future)

Perfect tenses—The forms of the verb that, in relation to time, show an action is perfected or completed. Past perfect was started and completed before some other action in the past. Present perfect started in the past and continues into the present or was started in the past and completed in the present. Future perfect will be completed by a specified time in the future.

Present infinitive—The word *to* joined to a present tense verb.

>I am able *to sing* now that my voice has returned.
>Debra will be able *to perform* the lead in tonight's play.
>Dave said that *to give* the news to the public is a great opportunity.

Present perfect infinitive—The words *to have* joined to the past participle form of the verb.

>I am pleased *to have been* of service to you during the past year.

>According to the latest report, Mr. Randall is happy *to have been* reassigned to his home town.

>We consider the opportunity *to have won* the race a great blessing.

Present perfect tense—The form of the verb that, in relation to time, points to something started in the past and continuing into the present or started in the past and completed in the present.

>After traveling for many hours, Brett *has arrived* at the front lobby.

Rachelle *has worked* on the files for many days, but she can finally see the end.
They *have served* on the committee for more than three years now.

Present tense—The base form of the verb that, in relation to time, points to something happening now, something done regularly or habitually, or something about to happen in the immediate future. The present tense is also used to express universal truths and the historical present.

If you *come* in now, I *can use* your assistance with my computer.
I *understand* the Fourth of July *is* not celebrated in Canada.

Progressive tense—The forms of the verb that, in relation to time, show an action or event in progress. Progressive tense verb forms consist of a form of *be* plus a present participle. This progression is illustrated in the following sentences:

Lynn *is seeing* all our customers. (present progressive)
Lynn *was seeing* all our customers. (past progressive)
Lynn *will be seeing* all our customers. (future progressive)
Lynn *has been seeing* all our customers. (present perfect progressive)
Lynn *had been seeing* all our customers. (past perfect progressive)
Lynn *will have been seeing* all our customers. (future perfect progressive)

Regular verb form—A verb that forms its past tense and past participle with *-d* or *-ed* added to the base form of the verb. For example:

Present tense	Past Tense	Past Participle
Now I . . .	Yesterday I . . .	In the past, I have . . .
analyze	analyzed	analyzed
complete	completed	completed
evaluate	evaluated	evaluated
review	reviewed	reviewed
report	reported	reported
try	tried	tried

Shift in tense—An illogical or unnecessary change from one verb tense to another within one sentence that results in confusion because the sequence of events as reflected in the verbs is unclear.

NOT: Bowen *represented* us at the convention but *wants* us to attend.
          Sabrina *will be representing* the company in Atlanta and *is seeing* her
              parents later.
          I know we *must have* a serious talk, and we *needed* to get problems in
              the open.

BUT: Bowen *represented* us at the convention but *wanted* us to attend.

Sabrina *will be representing* the company in Atlanta and *will be* seeing her parents later.

I know we *must have* a serious talk, and we *need* to get problems in the open.

Simple tenses—Present, past, and future tenses. The simple tenses do not include the perfect tenses or the progressive tenses.

Last Monday, I *tried* to get John to attend his classes. (past tense)

I *want* to do my best work on this assignment. (present tense)

Next Friday, I *will try* again to pass the examination. (future tense)

Transitive verb—A verb that requires an object to complete its meaning.

We *paid* our bills this morning.

I *drove* the truck all night to get here on time this morning.

Ms. Carson *began* the meeting promptly at 9 a.m.

Universal truth—A known statement of fact that uses the present tense.

The speaker said Hawaii *is* the fiftieth state admitted to the union.

The lead in last night's play *is* Mike's sister.

Although often overlooked, principles of ethics *are* important in business transactions.

Verbal—Verb forms (gerunds, participles, and infinitives) used as nouns, adjectives, or adverbs. Verbals may take objects, complements, and modifiers. Infinitives may have subjects. Examples are included with the definitions of *gerunds, infinitives,* and *participles.*

RULES

> **1. Use *present tense* to describe an action that is happening in the present or to describe a condition that exists at the present time.**

Mary *works* in fashion merchandising on the fifth floor.

Kent *needs* your assistance if you can spare the time.

Learning Tip 1: Use the present tense to indicate a customary action regardless of the other verbs in the sentence.

When the president *speaks*, members of the council listen.

Kate *leaves* her house promptly at 7:35 to catch the 7:40 bus.

Learning Tip 2: Use the present tense to express a universal truth, a continuing truth, or a relatively permanent truth regardless of when the truth was stated.

Despite what she said, 12 squared *is* 144.

The keynote speaker at yesterday's session indicated moral standards *are* still important.

Upon entering the hospital, Mr. Byers was informed his relative *is* dead.

Learning Tip 3: Use a dependent-clause verb that agrees in tense with the verb in the independent clause unless a universal truth is expressed in the subordinate clause.

Unfortunately, he *is* correct because he *is* the one who misjudged.

Last night, Elaine *said* she *was* going to start looking for a job; but this morning she has changed her mind.

Being from Colorado, he *knew* the 24th of July *is* celebrated in Utah.

Learning Tip 4: Be consistent in presenting the *historical present viewpoint* in your writing. Historical present is used when we write about happenings in a work of literature or when we quote or paraphrase someone who wrote a letter, an article, a book, etc. Novice writers have a tendency to write about such events in the past tense. The novice writer reasons that if the happening has already been written about, it must have happened in the past.

Such incidents are best written about in the present tense. In literature, the rationale for the present tense is that the happenings of literature are unchangeable and therefore are permanently true. The next time we read the play, Hamlet will kill Claudius just like the last time we read the play. Or in an article in *Business Week*, the article and the author's thinking still exist in their present form and are unaffected by time. For example:

In her article, Ms. Shelton *states* ratification of the treaty may be questionable.

I'm quoting President Warnick, who *indicates* the time is ripe for reform.

2. **Use *past tense* to describe an action or state of being that occurred some time in the past.**

At yesterday's session, Mr. Abraham *made* an offensive remark.

The shipment *was delivered* early this morning.

The secretary *arrived* just in time to record the opening remarks.

Learning Tip 5: To help you determine the verb form that should be used in the sentence, determine if the verb is transitive or intransitive. A transitive verb requires a direct object to complete its meaning. An intransitive verb does not require a direct object. For example:

I *lay* down last night for a rest after dinner. (*Lay* is the past tense form of *lie*, an intransitive verb that does not require an object.)

I *lay* the books on the table. (*Lay* is the present tense, a transitive verb that requires an object.)

She *sat* down to rest her weary bones. (*Sat* is the past tense of *sit*, an intransitive verb that does not require an object.)

He *set* the books on the table. (*Set* is both the present and past tense of *set*, a transitive verb that requires an object.)

3. **Use *future tense* to indicate an action to take place some time in the future or a state or condition that will exist some time in the future.**

According to the program, Tracy *will speak* in the Everglades Room at 3 p.m.

Tomorrow, you *shall be* on time for your first class.

If you are to succeed, you *will want* to set some realistic goals.

Learning Tip 6: Form future tense by placing *will* or *shall* before the verb.

Contrary to the past when specific instances dictated the use of *shall* or *will*, in today's language usage, *will* is typically used to express ordinary future tense; and *shall* is used to express a demand or is used with laws, policies, or contracts.

You *shall have* this assignment submitted on time.

Supervisors *shall ensure* the stated policies are implemented according to schedule.

If you meet the deadline, you *will reap* the reward.

4. **Use *present perfect tense* to describe an action started in the past and just completed or an action begun in the past and continuing into the present.**

Present perfect tense is formed by adding *has* or *have* to the past participle.

I *have been* occupying this office for the past 16 years.

After several hours, the building *has* finally *been* evacuated.

Only one worker *has worked* continually during the Mayor's administration.

5. **Use *past perfect tense* to indicate that the action or condition described by the verb was completed earlier than some other action that also occurred in the past.**

Past perfect tense is formed by adding *had* to the past participle.

We *had shipped* before we asked the postal service to put a trace on it.

Mr. Warren *had committed* himself before he made the appointment.

Before I reached my office, Lisa *had returned* my call.

6. **Use *future perfect tense* to name an action or condition that will be completed by some specified time in the future.**

Future perfect tense is formed by adding *shall have* or *will have* to the past participle.

By the end of the summer, Wood Manufacturing *will have completed* its new building.

Mr. Davis *will have been employed* by our company for 25 years in December.

Ms. Stockton *shall have entered* all data for your report by Monday.

A participle is a verb form used as an adjective that often ends with *-ing* or *-ed*.

A *present participle* is formed by adding *-ing* to the verb and is used to describe the present viewpoint. Examples include *using, making,* and *remembering*.

A *perfect participle* is formed by adding the word *having* to the past participle. Examples include *having finished, having paid*, and *having written*.

Learning Tip 7: Use the *present participle* to refer to action happening at the same time as the action of the main verb.

> *Finishing* first in the race, Sue *breaks* the tape.

> *Taking* his place in line, Jeffrey patiently *waits*.

Learning Tip 8: Literary writing uses the *present participle* to refer to action happening described in Learning Tip 7. However, because business writing is not as descriptive as literary writing, the verb in the main clause is often expressed in past tense even though the present participle is used.

> *Entering* the secured area, Manuel *presented* his security pass.

> *Running* to the window, I *saw* the elderly woman slip on the ice.

Learning Tip 9: Use the *perfect participle* to refer to action occurring before the action of the main verb. As in the following sentences, the perfect participle is often used to express a cause-effect relationship.

> *Having completed* her analysis, Dr. Wiseman *prepared* to leave her office.

> *Having served* his appointment, Mr. Aidukaitis *asked* to be reassigned.

A *present infinitive* consists of *to* plus a present-tense verb. Examples are *to be, to write,* and *to join*.

> We are waiting for Jennie *to go* to the store before we prepare the surprise.

We are able *to succeed* because we place the customer's needs first.

A *perfect infinitive* consists of *to* plus *have* plus a past participle. Examples are *to have studied, to have completed,* and *to have been.*

Julia is delighted *to have passed* the examination.

I am sorry *to have missed* the deadline.

Learning Tip 10: A present infinitive is conventionally used when the main verb is in the past or past perfect tense. Although a perfect infinitive might be logical with some main verbs in the past tense to show the time in the infinitive preceded the time in the main verb, present infinitives are consistently used in all exercises in *Practical Grammar Review.*

NOT: I was glad to have completed the examination before noon.

I wanted to have been a teaching aide during my junior year.

Morton had expected to have finished the project before you arrived.

BUT: I was glad to complete the examination before noon.

I wanted to be a teaching aide during my junior year.

Morton had expected to finish the project before you arrived.

Learning Tip 11: The word *had* should never be included in an infinitive.

NOT: As we thought, Al expected *to had been* invited to submit a proposal.

We desired *to had attended* the opening ceremonies.

Debbie was pleased *to had been selected* rodeo queen.

BUT: As we thought, Al had expected *to be* invited to submit a proposal.

We desired *to attend* the opening ceremonies.

Debbie was pleased *to be selected* rodeo queen.

Learning Tip 12: Do not write sentences in which both the main verb and the infinitive are preceded by *has, have,* or *had.*

NOT: I would have liked to have seen Jane before she left town.

We had expected to have overhauled the engine before it threw a rod.

BUT: I would have liked to see Jane before she left town.

We had expected to overhaul the engine before it threw a rod.

---

9.   Avoid unnecessary shifts in tense within a sentence.

A *shift* occurs when the writer changes one tense to another within a sentence. If the relationship of the tenses is not logical, an *illogical* shift has resulted, causing confusion to the reader. Analyze the *NOT* examples below to note this illogical shift; then, read the *BUT* examples to see how these sentences avoid this shift.

NOT: As you recall, yesterday we *reviewed* the contract and *will mail* it to her attorney.

The director *has come* to the meeting and *wanted* to see all sales personnel immediately.

Ron *will be presenting* the findings next month and *is going* to indicate our recommendations.

BUT: As you recall, yesterday we *reviewed* the contract and *mailed* it to her attorney.

The director *has come* to the meeting and *wants* to see all sales personnel immediately.

Ron *will be presenting* the findings next month and *will be indicating* our recommendations.

TENSE SELF-EVALUATION

Write *C* if the sentence is correct; write *I* if the sentence is incorrect. Compare your answers with those on the following page. For each item you missed, review the explanation and, if necessary, study the material again.

_____ 1. At last week's commencement, Mr. Majors indicated ethics were important for all graduates.

_____ 2. Your first major assignment will be due tomorrow.

_____ 3. Finished the project, she was completely exhausted.

_____ 4. I appreciate the opportunity to have served you in the past.

_____ 5. If you can meet with me now, I will be able to find the time.

_____ 6. Mr. Hill has been a keynote speaker for several conventions before he retired from public life.

_____ 7. If you are to succeed with this project, you will have to gain self-confidence.

_____ 8. Yesterday, Edwin comes into my office and complained of discrimination.

_____ 9. By Christmas, I will complete the first draft of my novel.

_____ 10. She wants to have finished the assignment by class tomorrow.

_____ 11. Suzanna is right when she said she will be here on time tomorrow.

_____ 12. The time of the session you missed yesterday is 9:30.

_____ 13. When Mr. Haroldson presides, committee members respond.

_____ 14. I had hoped to have finished all tax returns long before now.

_____ 15. When I see the film, I feel ill.

_____ 16. In her article, Ms. Fox indicates the issue is not as obvious as most people believe.

_____ 17. Having committed herself to the task, Marsha had requested my assistance.

_____ 18. The computer had been shipped before the software had been received.

ANSWERS TO TENSE SELF-EVALUATION

1. I   Use present tense for statements of universal truth. (Rule 1; LT2)

2. C   *Will be* is correctly used in future tense. (Rule 3)

3. I   Use the perfect participle, *having finished*, to show action occurring before the action of the main verb. (Rule 7; LT9)

4. C   Use the present perfect infinitive with an action occurring before the action of the main verb. (Rule 8; LT13)

5. I   Use the present tense verb, *can find*, to show events in the present time frame. (Rule 1)

6. I   Use *had been* with past perfect tense to show an action completed before another action. (Rule 5)

7. C   Use the present form of the infinitive with present tense. (Rule 8; LT11)

8. I   Avoid tense shifts from present to past tense. (Rule 9)

9. I   Use future perfect *will have completed* to indicate a continuing action to be completed at a specified time in the future. (Rule 6)

10. I   Use the present infinitive *to finish* with present tense. (Rule 8; LT12)

11. I   Use the same tense in the subordinate clause and in the main clause. (Rule 1; LT3)

12. I   Use simple past tense *was* to describe events in the past. (Rule 2)

13. C   Use the present tense to indicate customary action. (Rule 1; LT1)

14. I   Use the present infinitive *to finish* with past perfect. (Rule 8; LT10)

15. C   Use present tense to indicate a present action. (Rule 1)

16. C   Use the present tense to present the present viewpoint. (Rule 1; LT4)

17. I   The perfect participle and the past perfect tense are both trying illogically to do the same thing—show that one event preceded the other. (LT9; Rule 5)

18. I   The two past perfect verbs are both trying illogically to do the same thing—show that both events were in the past and that one occurred before the other. (Rule 5)

Write *T* if the statement is true; write *F* if the statement is false.

____   1.   Past tense describes actions that occurred in the past.

____   2.   Regardless of the viewpoint, the lead-in to a quotation from a published source is written in past tense.

____   3.   The present participle is formed when the writer adds *-ing* to the verb. The present participle is used to describe the present viewpoint.

____   4.   A relatively permanent truth is expressed in past tense.

____   5.   Use future perfect tense to name an action to be completed at an unknown future time.

____   6.   The present infinitive is used when the main action is in the present tense.

____   7.   Literary writing typically uses the past participle to refer to an action happening at the same time as that of the main verb.

____   8.   An action started in the past and just now completed uses the past perfect tense.

____   9.   An infinitive used in a sentence depicting future tense typically contains *have* and *been* between *to* and the verb.

____   10.   A future action that designates a specific completion time should be the future perfect tense.

____   11.   Form future tense by writing *will* or *shall* before the verb.

____   12.   When an infinitive is used in a sentence in which an action occurs before the action of the main verb, the present form of the infinitive is used.

____   13.   Use the present participle to refer to an action happening at the same time as the action of the main verb.

____   14.   A shift in tense in a sentence is no problem if the writer uses a conjunctive adverb.

____   15.   The present form of the infinitive is used in sentences in present and future tense but not in past tense.

____   16.   Past perfect tense is formed with *had* plus the past participle.

____   17.   Present perfect tense is formed with *has* or *have* plus the present participle.

TENSE EXERCISE 2

Name_____

Write *C* to indicate the sentence is correct; write *I* to indicate the sentence is incorrect. Underline the subject of each clause once; underline the verb or verb phrase of each clause twice; and then bracket each dependent clause.

_____ 1. For past conferences, we decided never to have asked a boring speaker to participate.

_____ 2. Next year, we will try again to win the basketball championship.

_____ 3. Each morning promptly at 7:32, I walked to the curb to catch my commuter van.

_____ 4. Please accept my suggestion to volunteer your time to our homeless shelter.

_____ 5. The order was shipped before our check had been cashed.

_____ 6. If you want to be happy, you must have been in control of your thoughts and actions.

_____ 7. Having received a letter from his girl friend, Willy requested the weekend off.

_____ 8. The news anchor presented a teaser to have enticed viewers to watch the news.

_____ 9. By Labor Day, Word Processors Inc. will have finished writing the documentation for its new product.

_____ 10. Jane admitted she was the contest's mystery woman.

_____ 11. Read the policy and sign on the line indicating that, in the future, you agree to abide by all stipulations.

_____ 12. Bill is pleased to have been able to participate in yesterday's conference.

_____ 13. After several hours of work, I have finally completed your tax return.

_____ 14. Yesterday, Professor Young indicated Mexico bordered four states of the union.

_____ 15. Completing the assignment, Robin sighs a sense of relief.

_____ 16. Having learned her lesson, Ng walks from the room.

_____ 17. Having seen the commotion, Wilma had thought about taking a different route home.

_____ 18. By the end of the semester, Stewart will have completed all his general education.

_____ 19. If you understood the situation, you would not have requested a leave of absence.

TENSE EXERCISE 3   Name_____

Write *A* if the first choice in parentheses is correct; write *B* if the second choice is correct.

_____ 1. I told him yesterday he (had/has) to understand that last night I couldn't think clearly.

_____ 2. Having completed her assignment, Sue (leaves/left) the library.

_____ 3. Overhearing the doctor's conversation, I realized the patient (is/was) dead.

_____ 4. By noon tomorrow, the report (will be/will have been) on your desk.

_____ 5. We wanted (to attend/to have attended) the opening ceremonies in Symphony Hall last night.

_____ 6. We (will/will have) filled your orders by closing time.

_____ 7. If you want (to drive/to have driven) to New Mexico, you must first learn to change a flat tire.

_____ 8. We (arrived/had arrived) just in time to see the fireworks.

_____ 9. When dictators (reign/have reigned) harshly, the people suffer.

_____10. We (agreed/had agreed) to the stipulations before the change order was received.

_____11. If you (are/can be) available, we can use your services now.

_____12. The book report (is/will be) due at the beginning of class next Thursday.

_____13. I am requesting you (to play/to have played) my favorite song.

_____14. (Turning/Having turned) off his computer and gathered his papers, Tom found additional data to input.

_____15. I (congratulate/have congratulated) you many times on your many accomplishments.

_____16. Benny was delighted (to be selected/to have been selected) for the assignment.

_____17. The owner of the Williams Lake resort (was/is) my uncle.

_____18. Celeste will eventually desire (to resign/to have resigned) from the committee.

_____19. Agreeing the procedures were correct, the auditors (elected/had elected) to proceed with the audit.

TENSE   69

Name_____

Read each sentence and note the verb choices in parentheses. On the line, write the number that indicates the correct tense:

    1 = past tense   4 = past perfect tense
    2 = present tense   5 = present perfect tense
    3 = future tense   6 = future perfect tense

_____ 1. We (are/were) waiting for Al to bring in the mail when you arrived.

_____ 2. Having already purchased the tickets, we (bypass/bypassed) the long line at the theater.

_____ 3. In her letter, Ms. Stewart instructs me to thank you for her (being able/having been able) to tutor you during the past year.

_____ 4. Entering the secured area, Mr. Youngston (inserts/inserted) his security code.

_____ 5. In my research paper, I quoted the president of Yale who (states/stated) tuition is increasing at Ivy League schools.

_____ 6. I (had been/have been) serving in this capacity for seven years.

_____ 7. Looking at the map, I noticed much of Maine (is/was) north of the Canadian border.

_____ 8. After working on my book for over a year, I (will complete/will have completed) it by this time next year.

_____ 9. Your duties tomorrow (include/will include) sweeping and dusting.

_____10. She (made/had made) the cookies for last night's social.

_____11. As of Memorial Day next month, you (have used/will have used) all your vacation time for the year.

_____12. Professor Young promised that tomorrow he (would have/will have) completed our assignments.

_____13. During the years I (had/have) known her, she has never reneged on her promises.

_____14. Before I left the office, the phone call (was/had been) returned.

_____15. Each morning promptly at 7:35, I (leave/left) the house.

_____16. The front matter of a dictionary (explains/will have explained) the entries.

Edit to correct all tense errors. Two of the sentences are correct.

1. Attention all cashiers: We needed your help at the front of the store.

2. A standard of ethics was needed by all employees to keep customers' trust.

3. By Christmas, all courses will have been successfully completed.

4. He came into my classroom and announces his intention to withdraw.

5. The news release quotes the company president, who indicated a small profit was earned during the first quarter.

6. Sobbing hysterically, she tells of the letter she just received.

7. Yesterday, we go shopping to buy a new spring suit.

8. I am occupying the chair for seven years.

9. In the 6:30 darkness of morning each day, my alarm rang.

10. Having completed the exam, she leaves before the bell rings.

11. I can say I am proud to have been an American.

12. After making her bed, she comes down to breakfast.

13. Tomorrow, Isaiah will have been glad to give his attention to his professor.

14. Everyone had hoped to have mastered the new software before you had returned.

Edit to correct all tense errors. Two of the sentences are correct.

1. We want to have been able to have increased income as well as improved public relations with this campaign.

2. After entering his four-digit code into the security system, Hideo pushes the door open and enters the vault.

3. Whether or not you procrastinate, your assignment is due Tuesday.

4. I'm sorry you're leaving; I've enjoyed the opportunity to be able to have served you for the past 17 years.

5. Having committed to have remained on the panel for three years, Ester feels guilty when she asks for a release.

6. Policy dictates you shall work on Saturdays next month.

7. Try to have completed and to have mailed your tax forms by midnight.

8. We have been trying now for several months to implement our promotion policy.

9. Last night, I read in the almanac that the Chinese New Year and our New Year's Day were not celebrated at the same time.

10. Even if you say you don't understand, you were involved.

11. Last Monday, my father indicates he is going to Tulsa next week.

12. Having sought the reasons for the errors, Mr. Boyd had requested my assistance.

MOOD AND VOICE

MOOD DISCUSSION

As you know, tense is the verb property that specifies when in time an action occurred. Another verb property is *mood*. Mood refers to the manner, or way, a statement is intended to be understood. That is, *mood* identifies the writer's specific message as it is expressed by the verb form.

Through our choice of mood, we can direct the reader to regard a comment as a statement of fact, a question, a command, a doubtful statement, a contrary-to-fact statement, an improbable statement, or an impossible statement. As writers, we select one of three moods to convey the manner in which ideas are to be understood.

1. The *indicative mood* is used to make a statement of fact or to ask a question.

2. The *imperative mood* is used to make a request or a strong recommendation, to offer a suggestion, or to give a command.

3. The *subjunctive mood* is used to express a wish, a statement of doubt, a recommendation, an improbability, an impossible statement, or a contrary-to-fact statement.

Indicative Mood

Verbs in the indicative mood are primarily used to make statements of fact or to ask questions about facts. However, writers must recognize that limiting the use of indicative mood just to making statements of fact or to asking questions is too restrictive. The indicative mood is also used to make statements of inference or assumption.

Some writers and readers erroneously assume that declarative statements are always statements of fact. The exact writer distinguishes between statements that are factual and those that are inferences or assumptions.

With the caution just noted, use of the indicative mood is very natural. Indicative-mood sentences are easy to identify and easy to understand.

Line charts show the movements or changes of a continuous series of data over time. (States a fact.)

Which of the three types of bar charts best illustrates these data? (Asks a simple question.)

Based on available evidence, the witness seems to have withheld information during the trial. (States an inference.)

Imperative Mood

Verbs in the imperative mood are used when we give instructions, give orders, or make certain kinds of requests. Note that the subject of a verb in the imperative mood is always *you* and is usually omitted or understood from the context.

Perhaps the most-frequent mistake we make is not using the imperative mood often enough. The imperative mood need not be rude or offensive when used for the right purpose. In fact, an order or a request stated in the imperative mood is usually not only emphatic but also quickly and easily understood. In addition, use of imperative mood is effective in policy and procedure statements.

Note how flexible the imperative mood is in creating easy-to-understand messages:

Use a courteous, professional tone in all your business dealings.
Read the instructions thoroughly before using the new video equipment.
Please let us know when you want your *Wall Street Journal* subscription to begin.
Tell Nina in the word-processing center to edit the final draft of the document.

Subjunctive Mood

In modern English and in business writing, the subjunctive mood has steadily decreased in usage. Still, the subjunctive mood is used to express doubtful, contrary-to-fact, improbable, or impossible conditions. We also use the subjunctive mood to make certain types of requests, to express wishes, to make recommendations, and to give indirect commands.

If his statement *were* true, we *would* have cause to be concerned.
The briefing was presented *as though* it *were* the final decision.
If Estella *could* accept a fee, she *would* be willing to make the speech.
If only Hui-li *were* able to start her MBA program this term, she *could* graduate with her husband.
I wish we *were* able to approve Danilo's transfer to Trujillo, Peru.
Graduate business programs *should* begin offering international courses.
Kira asked that a committee *be* appointed to study the Hess case.

The verbs *were* and *be* frequently signal subjunctive intent. Also, helping verbs *may*, *might*, and *ought* set up the subjunctive mood. Notice also that *should, would,* and *could* statements are in the subjunctive mood.

Illustrations

Note the tone created in each of the following statements when a different mood is illustrated.

Indicative Mood

The present method used to distribute student tickets to athletic events is inefficient. Therefore, a student committee has been assigned to develop an improved plan by April 29. The new plan, hopefully, will eliminate many of the present priority and discrimination problems. Most important, however, is the fact that the students will have had a major voice in the decision process.

Imperative Mood

Reduce the inefficiency in the basketball-ticket-distribution process by developing a new, innovative plan. Assign a student committee to study the current process and to recommend a new plan that gives priority to currently enrolled students. Please have the committee present its recommendations by April 29. To avoid possible discrimination, make certain the students' concerns are fully considered.

Subjunctive Mood

If each student were permitted to express his or her feelings about the present basketball-ticket-distribution system, disagreement would still exist. The administration suggests that a student committee be organized to discuss ways to change the current procedures. The committee should present its recommendations by April 29. By the way, if I were on the committee, I would be concerned about the priority and discrimination problems that have been reported.

Conclusion—In business writing, a decision reached after facts have been analyzed. Conclusions are inferences stated in indicative mood.

> Students desire and deserve a voice in how athletic tickets are distributed.

Finding—A statement reporting phenomena or observations without interpretation. In business writing, findings are stated in indicative mood.

> Seventy-two percent of the student body participated in the ticket survey.

Imperative mood—A statement that gives a command, makes a request, or provides directions. In business writing, policy or procedure directives are commonly stated in imperative mood. Recommendations are sometimes stated in imperative mood, especially when the writer wants the tone to be absolute or without any feeling of doubt.

> Appoint a student committee to review the ticket-distribution procedure.

Indicative mood—A statement of fact or a question. In business writing, a majority of sentences are in indicative mood.

> Junior, senior, and graduate students attended the forum to express their feelings about how to distribute tickets for campus events.
> Will you report the committee findings at the next staff meeting?

Mood—The form of the verb used to indicate an intended meaning to be understood by an expression or by an action. English usage has indicative, imperative, and subjunctive moods.

Recommendation—A statement of counsel or advice indicating something be done. Business recommendations are frequently expressed through the subjunctive *should*. The intent is to suggest an action, leaving the decision to the reader.

> The executive council should write the ticket-distribution policy to be included in next year's catalog.

If the writer wants to eliminate any doubt about the action to be taken, an imperative-mood recommendation may be appropriate.

> Direct the executive council to write the ticket-distribution policy for next year's catalog.

Subjunctive mood—A statement that reflects a wish, a doubtful statement, a contrary-to-fact condition, an improbable situation, or an impossible situation.

I wish the students were in complete agreement on this issue.

I would give you a ticket to the game if I had an extra one.

If the student officers were experienced, they could write the ticket policy.

RULES FOR MOOD

1. Use the indicative mood to make a statement of fact or to ask a question.

The entire staff was present when the announcement was made.

Are you planning to attend the communication convention in Atlanta this October?

When the news report is released, will we be expected to make a public statement?

Learning Tip 1: In if/then statements, indicative mood can be used when the writer considers the *if* statement to be true or probable. In indicative-mood if/then statements, the verbs *was* and *is* (rather than *were* and *be*) are used with *will*, *can*, and *shall* (rather than *would*, *could*, and *should*). For example:

If the report *is* correct, we *will* have to purchase additional equipment.

If the shipment of parts *was* received on time, we *can* expect to complete the project by the end of the month.

Learning Tip 2: In business writing, conclusions and decisions are usually stated in indicative mood. Conclusions are logical inferences based on facts or findings that suggest what data mean to the writer.

Diversity of students in business classes contributes best to program internationalization.

Students desire an active role when educators modify course content and instructional design.

2. Use the imperative mood to express a command, make a request, make a suggestion, or give directions.

In *Practical Grammar Review*, the subject of all imperative-mood clauses is the understood *you*.

Drive carefully on your way home.

Always place the protective covering over your computer when you leave work.
Send letters of appointment to the applicants who will begin working for us next month.
Read the instructions carefully before assembling your computer.

Learning Tip 3: The imperative mood is effective when rules are stated. The imperative mood is also effective when policies or procedures are stated.

Return motor-pool vehicle keys to the main office at the close of each workday.
Lock all file cabinets and office doors before leaving your work area.
Submit medical claims within ten days after being treated by your primary-care physician.

Learning Tip 4: When you use imperative mood, you may want to soften the message by improving the tone. One way to improve tone in imperative-mood statements is to include the word *please* along with the verb.

Return the questionnaire in the enclosed envelope by April 30.
Please return the questionnaire in the enclosed envelope by April 30.

Lock the safe before you leave the office this evening.
Please lock the safe before you leave the office this evening.

You may also use imperative mood to make a request when *please* is not needed to improve the message tone.

Let us help you implement this program in your firm.

Learning Tip 5: Recommendations are sometimes stated in imperative mood when the writer wants to assure the tone leaves no doubt about the importance of an action.

Include at least 25 percent international students in business classes to promote global understanding of the issues.
Reduce overhead expenses by not replacing employees who retire or who leave the company for other employment.

3. Use the subjunctive mood to make statements you think are untrue, impossible, or improbable.

NOT: If I *was* you, I would counsel your staff writer to eliminate redundant words and unnecessary repetition.

BUT: If I *were* you, I would counsel your staff writer to eliminate redundant words and unnecessary repetition.

Learning Tip 6: If/then statements are usually expressed in subjunctive mood because the writer believes the statements to be untrue, impossible, or improbable. In subjunctive if/then statements, the subjunctive verbs *were* and *be* (rather than *was* and *is*) are used with *would*, *could*, and *should* (rather than *will, can,* and *shall*).

If I *were* elected treasurer, I *could* try to reduce taxes.
If Danica *were* assigned to the Lubbock office, she *should* make the presentation.
If this report *be* true, we *would* do well to change our operating policy.

Learning Tip 7: The expressions *as if, as though,* and *I wish* are always subjunctive because they mean "not really, but supposing that . . . ."

Andres spoke *as if* he were in favor of writing a marketing proposal.
The marketing proposal was presented *as though* it represented the board's final decision.
I wish you were able to participate in the tour to Israel this spring.

Learning Tip 8: Occasionally, past-tense verbs used to express present or future events create the subjunctive mood.

If I *revealed* the projected merger dates, I would be fired.
If I *told* you all I know about the project, you would be amazed.

Learning Tip 9: Expressing requests or making indirect commands are also part of subjunctive-mood usage.

We suggest a task force *be* assigned to consider the plan.
I insist you *be* with me at the briefing.

Learning Tip 10: The subjunctive *should* is often used to make recommendations in business writing. The subjunctive usage for recommendations is appropriate because the writer has no assurance the reader will implement the advice or suggestions given.

Students should preregister for classes before November 15 to avoid a late-registration fee.
Executives should select bilingual employees for international assignments.

Learning Tip 11: The subjunctive *would* is often used to express a customary action:

In the fall, we would go hunting almost every weekend.

In good business writing and in *Practical Grammar Review*, however, such usage of the subjunctive *would* is incorrect. One function of subjunctive mood is to express doubt, and some writers feel the subjunctive *would* expresses doubt incorrectly. Therefore, we recommend that you reserve the subjunctive *would* for those situations clearly requiring the subjunctive mood and that you use the indicative or imperative moods in other situations.

NOT: I would like to tell you about my business background.
        We would appreciate hearing from you by May 10.
        We would ask you to keep this matter confidential.

BUT: I will tell you about my business background.
        Please let us hear from you by May 10.
        We ask you to keep this matter confidential.

4. Avoid illogical shifts in mood within a sentence.

When writing, be consistent in your point of view. Most illogical mood shifts are indicative-imperative shifts, but other shifts also occur. A shift in mood is confusing to the reader because it suggests the writer has changed his or her way of looking at conditions.

NOT: *Assign* an identification number to each employee, and then you *can prepare* a list of all employee names and numbers. (imperative-indicative shift)

BUT: *Assign* an identification number to each employee, and then *prepare* a list of all employee names and numbers. (imperative-imperative)

NOT: A report of the proceedings *should be* prepared, and Susan *plans* to distribute copies to the faculty. (subjunctive-indicative shift)

BUT: A report of the proceedings *should be* prepared, and copies *should be* distributed to the faculty. (subjunctive-subjunctive)

VOICE DISCUSSION

Voice is another property of verbs. To understand voice, we must know the distinction between active and passive voice. However, we must avoid the mistake of thinking that every verb is either active or passive. Some verbs are neither active nor passive but are known as state-of-being or linking verbs.

Voice indicates whether the subject of the verb is performing or receiving the action described by the verb. Two common directives are:

1. Use active voice to emphasize the performer of an action.

2. Use passive voice to de-emphasize the performer of the action—thereby emphasizing the object of the action.

If the subject is the doer of the action, the accompanying verb is called *active*—and the sentence is in the *active voice*. On the other hand, if the subject is being acted upon, the accompanying verb is called *passive*—and the sentence is in the *passive voice*.

Although "rules" are associated with the illustration of voice, they are really options you can choose to create the syntax or the meaning you wish. Depending upon your audience purpose, you can decide whether to use active voice or passive voice. Your ability to use voice principles effectively will increase if you understand the difference between transitive and intransitive verbs. (See Tense Rule 2.)

However, good advice in business writing is *prefer active voice to passive voice*.

TERMINOLOGY FOR VOICE

Active voice—Results when the sentence subject performs the action indicated by the verb. Active voice emphasizes the performer of the action.

> *Kristan used* effective visuals in her presentation.

Intransitive verb—A verb that does not require an object to complete its meaning.

> I *notice* that Mary Ann drives on the left side of the road.

Linking verb—A verb that connects the subject with the subject complement. The various forms of *to be* are the linking verbs and are often called *state-of-being verbs*. However, some linking verbs are not considered state-of-being verbs—*appear, become, feel, look, remain, seem, smell, sound,* and *taste*.

> Mr. Hamilton *is* an honest person.
> When in Israel, you will find the bread *tastes* especially good.

Passive voice—Results when the subject is acted upon or receives the action and is formed by a state-of-being helping verb plus a past-participle helping verb. Passive voice emphasizes the object of the action.

An excellent presentation *was made* by Morris at this morning's staff briefing.

Past participle—A verb that usually ends in *-ed* for regular verbs or that is formed irregularly as listed in the tense section and that cannot function as a predicate without a helper. A state-of-being helping verb plus a past-participle main verb forms the passive voice.

> We have *worked* on the report all morning.
> We are *committed* to Ms. Ames.

State-of-being verb—Forms of the verb *be* (*am, is, are, was, were, be, been, being*). State-of-being verbs are also called *linking verbs*.

> The consensus *is* that international students *are* intelligent and industrious.

Subject complement—A noun, pronoun, or adjective that follows an intransitive linking verb and that completes the meaning of the verb.

> Alisa is *independent*.

Transitive verb—A verb that requires an object to complete its meaning.

> Matt *sent* the proposal by express mail yesterday.

Voice—The verb property that indicates whether the subject performs the action or whether the subject receives the action. A verb with a direct object is in the *active voice*. When the direct object becomes the sentence subject, the verb is in the *passive voice*.

> Michael *manages* the graduate communication program.
> The graduate communication program *is managed* by Michael.

RULES FOR VOICE

5. Use active voice to show the subject performs the action in the sentence.

When a verb is in the active voice, the subject of the clause is the performer of the action. When you write business messages, use active voice whenever you can because it is more direct and is clearer than passive voice.

> **NOT:** The budget proposal will be reviewed by the board of directors and will be voted upon at the next meeting. (The writer wishes to place emphasis on the people performing the action.)

MOOD AND VOICE

BUT: The board of directors will review the budget proposal and will vote on it at the next meeting.

When a verb is in the passive voice, the subject is acted upon by the verb.

NOT: The committee prepared the budget statement improperly. (The writer wishes to focus attention on the condition of the budget statement rather than to accuse the committee.)

BUT: The budget statement was prepared improperly.

Learning Tip 12: We form passive voice by using the past participle of the verb plus a state-of-being helping verb (*am, is, are, was, were, be, been, being*). Therefore, to determine if a verb is passive, look for a state-of-being helping verb plus the past-participle form of the verb.

> Passive = State-of-being helping verb + Past-participle main verb

For example: The bell *was + rung* and the students *were + dismissed*.

The computer *was + programmed* soon after it *was + installed*.

Another way to determine if a clause is passive is to add the phrase "by [someone]" following the verb. Passive-voice clauses will still make sense—or sound right—when the "by [someone]" is added.

> Passive = State-of-being helping verb + "by someone"

For example: The bell *was rung + (by the principal)*, and the students *were dismissed + (by the teacher)*.

The computer *was programmed + (by the staff)* soon after it *was installed + (by the manufacturer)*.

Note how tone can be improved by using passive voice.

Active: **You** failed to enclose the questionnaire.
Passive: The questionnaire was not enclosed.

7. **Use a linking verb to express a condition that requires neither active nor passive voice.**

Linking verbs are neither active nor passive. They are always intransitive and therefore never have objects. *Be* verbs are also known as state-of-being verbs and sometimes are referred to as "no-action" verbs because no one does anything or because nothing is acted upon when they are used.

Notice in the terminology for voice that the linking-verb list includes the usual state-of-being verbs (*am, is, are, was, were, be, been,* and *being*) plus the sense verbs (*appear, become, feel, look, remain, seem, smell, sound,* and *taste*).

I *am* the supervisor today.
An alert receptionist always *appears* gracious and friendly.
Few citizens *are* aware of the report's implications.
Tiffin *felt* confident before and during the interview.

Use of a state-of-being verb as a main verb creates a situation that is neither active voice nor passive voice. State-of-being verbs as main verbs tell what the subjects *are, were,* or *will be*. State-of-being verbs are also known as *linking verbs* because they link a subject complement to the subject of the verb.

8. **Avoid illogical shifts in voice within sentences.**

You have already studied illogical shifts in tense and mood. Within a sentence, shifts in voice also can be distracting or even confusing to a reader. Although shifts in voice might occur within paragraphs, we usually focus attention on avoiding voice shifts in complex or in compound sentences. Following are examples of inappropriate shifts in voice:

NOT: The *agenda will be posted* outside the conference room, and the *secretary will send* a reminder to everyone. (passive-active shift)

BUT: The *agenda will be posted* outside the conference room, and a *reminder will be sent* to everyone. (passive-passive)

NOT: The *class members discussed* the project thoroughly, but none of the *reports were turned* in on time. (active-passive shift)

BUT: The *class members discussed* the project thoroughly, but *they did not turn* in any of the reports on time. (active-active)

MOOD AND VOICE SELF-EVALUATION

Write *C* if the sentence is correct; write *I* if the sentence is incorrect. Compare your answers with those on the answer sheet. For each item you missed, review the explanation and, if necessary, study the material again.

_____ 1. I wish your administrative assistant were errorless in his proofreading.

_____ 2. The supervisor reviewed the material, but no recommendations were announced.

_____ 3. If your report was already completed, the review could be ready by Friday.

_____ 4. The report writer was reminded by her supervisor that graphic aids are placed near the data being illustrated.

_____ 5. A pie chart is used whenever percentage comparison of variables is needed; use a line chart, however, to show the movements of a continuous series of data over time.

_____ 6. The writer used the deductive method in her report to place emphasis on the conclusions and on the plan of action.

_____ 7. Which form will you use to list the surplus inventory items?

_____ 8. The policy manual is accurate and up to date.

_____ 9. Begin studying the firm for which you eventually desire to work.

_____ 10. You should attend the meetings regularly. [The writer wants to express a command.]

_____ 11. If he was the senator from Wyoming, he would vote for the legislation.

_____ 12. We cannot approve the refund you requested. [Passive voice is desired to de-emphasize the performer of the action.]

_____ 13. The students are knowledgeable about the bill's implications. [Active voice is desired]

_____ 14. The company needs to give each time-card worker a 5 percent increase in salary this year. [A recommendation is desired.]

_____ 15. If the report about street crime is true, we will have to reassess safety when traveling.

_____ 16. I would like to give you some advice.

_____ 17. As your supervisor, I would ask you for your support.

ANSWERS TO MOOD AND VOICE SELF-EVALUATION

1. C   Subjunctive *were* is correct because the performance is not errorless. (Rule 3)

2. I   The sentence reflects a shift in voice from active voice *supervisor received* to passive voice *recommendations were announced*. (Rule 8)

3. I   *Was* is incorrect because the statement is contrary to fact and therefore requires subjunctive mood. The subjunctive use of *could* is correct. (Rule 3)

4. C   Passive *was reminded* is consistent with passive *are placed*. (Rule 6)

5. I   The mood shift is from indicative to imperative. The voice shift is from passive to active. (Rule 4; Rule 8)

6. C   Active voice *writer used* is correctly used to show the subject is performing the action in the sentence. (Rule 5)

7. C   Use indicative mood to ask a simple question. (Rule 1)

8. C   The verb is a *no-action linking verb* that reflects state of being. (Rule 7)

9. C   The imperative mood is used to make a suggestion. (Rule 2)

10. I   The imperative mood, not the subjunctive mood, is used to express a command: *Please attend the meetings regularly*. (Rule 2)

11. I   The subjunctive "If he *were* the senator . . ." must be used to show a condition that is contrary to fact. (Rule 3)

12. I   Passive voice is *The refund cannot be given to you*. (Rule 6)

13. I   The verb is a state-of-being verb rather than an active-voice verb. (Rule 5)

14. I   Replace *needs* with *should* to change the statement of fact or conclusion to a recommendation. (Rule 3; LT10)

15. C   If/then statements using *is* are indicative mood. (LT1)

16. I   The expression of doubt through the subjunctive *would* is unnecessary. (LT11)

17. I   Indicative *I ask* is preferred to subjunctive *I would ask.* (LT11)

MOOD AND VOICE

MOOD AND VOICE EXERCISE 3   Name_____

Write *A* if the first choice is correct; write *B* if the second choice is correct.

_____ 1. I wish this assignment (was/were) not due until Monday.

_____ 2. Please order a new laser printer from PRINTCO, and then (arrange/you should plan) an orientation seminar for the office staff.

_____ 3. Heidi said that if she (was/were) Steven, she would request a transfer.

_____ 4. If Shawna is ill tomorrow, will Tanya attend the meeting in her place? [indicative mood/subjunctive mood]

_____ 5. a. The boss told us to not bother him again today.
           b. The boss was definitely irritable today. [intent: to express a condition requiring neither active nor passive voice]

_____ 6. a. Our receptionist, Marjorie, placed the telephone call.
           b. The telephone call was placed by Marjorie, our receptionist. [intent: to emphasize who performed the action]

_____ 7. a. A 30 percent increase in sales during July was reflected in the report.
           b. The speaker described a 30 percent increase in July's sales. [intent: to stress the action performed]

_____ 8. If their bid (be/is) low, I would be very surprised.

_____ 9. The office definitely will close early on Thanksgiving. [imperative mood/indicative mood]

_____ 10. Please notify Brett of his transfer to the St. Louis branch. [imperative mood/subjunctive mood)

_____ 11. The writing team completed its task; however, none of the participants [were pleased with/liked] the results.

_____ 12. As expected, the defense attorney requested that she [question/questions] our client immediately.

_____ 13. Prepare the new sick-leave guidelines, and [have them distributed/distribute them] to all employees.

MOOD AND VOICE   91

MOOD AND VOICE EXERCISE 4   Name_____

Write the letters that match each sentence with the mood and voice used in the sentence: *A*—indicative mood, *B*—imperative mood, *C*—subjunctive mood, *AV*—active voice, *PV*—passive voice, or *LV*—state-of-being or linking verbs.

_____ 1. Let us help you complete your tax return.

_____ 2. We would appreciate your forwarding this proposal to marketing division promptly.

_____ 3. The racquetballs were delivered to the participants yesterday.

_____ 4. Avoid including any embarrassing information on your electronic-mail system.

_____ 5. Users of our electronic-mail system carefully edit their electronic-mail messages.

_____ 6. The privacy issues were agreed to by both parties in the dispute.

_____ 7. You should not have mentioned my comments from the board meeting.

_____ 8. Hospital care would not be caring or compassionate without service volunteers.

_____ 9. No communication links are available in the Glacier Park canyon areas.

_____10. Angela's nomination as Phi Kappa Phi vice president was recommended by Cheryl.

_____11. Classify each of your deductions in its correct category.

_____12. We should have sent the refund before the 15th of May.

_____13. You should have been honest in your dealings with your clients.

_____14. Tell Kristy to go to the benefits office before the beginning of the month.

_____15. The criteria for candidate selection were developed by Mr. Thorstensen.

_____16. Richard's analyses about computer back-up files are correct.

_____17. Don't put any confidential information on your electronic-mail system.

_____18. Consider how important George's being on time is to your success.

_____19. Close the vault and set the alarm system as you leave.

Write the letter identifying the one best answer.

_____ 1. a.   I have enclosed the camera-ready copy you requested in your last letter. [The writer wishes to de-emphasize the performer of the action.]
      b.   Today's meeting should be limited to 30 minutes.   [The writer wishes to emphasize the object receiving the action.]
      c.   The personnel director was asked to submit his resignation before the end of the month. [The writer wishes to emphasize the performer of the action.]

_____ 2. a.   Will you take the CPA exam this summer?
      b.   If she was to do that, we would cancel the contract. [highly improbable]
      c.   If that is to occur, we would have to cut production in half. [probable]

_____ 3. a.   Analyze the recommendations, and I will have them put into effect right away.
      b.   I will approve a discount, and then we should make an appropriate entry in the ledger.
      c.   Telephone the bank, report the error, and go home.

_____ 4. a.   Send the report to the Boston office; keep the documentation on file here.
      b.   A summary of our recommendations will be prepared, and we will distribute copies to the committee members.
      c.   As Deana searched through the files, the missing report was found.

_____ 5. a.   Give me that report, and you shouldn't submit it with so many errors.
      b.   Review the program and submit your analysis by noon tomorrow.
      c.   Please submit a complete financial report; and when the report is submitted, you may call a board meeting to review the figures.

_____ 6. a.   The plant superintendent wishes he were eligible for retirement.
      b.   The office manager, Mr. Dunston, wishes he was not going to be transferred.
      c.   The associate manager wishes he was going to be placed in charge of distribution as well as of production.

_____ 7. a.   When we receive the approved quotation, arrangements can be made to issue the purchase order.
      b.   Henry is the person, I understand, who needs the sabbatical leave the most.
      c.   The office manager approved the procedures; the new policy was approved by the executive vice president.

MOOD AND VOICE EXERCISE 6   Name_____

Write the letter identifying any correct sentences. Some items may have more than one answer.

_____ 1.   a.   Copyright law for quoting journal references and for copying software is clear.
           b.   Timm's latest novel is being praised by the intelligence community.
           c.   Most members of the Wasatch Book Club are complimentary of Timm's new book.

_____ 2.   a.   I wish he were the operations manager.
           b.   If I were you, I would ask for an extension of my contract.
           c.   If inflation was to occur, we would have to cut production in half. [improbable]

_____ 3.   a.   We will reach a conclusion, and a recommendation should be proposed.
           b.   Before a vote is taken, further discussion of the motion is needed.
           c.   Sign and date your tax return; then mail the return in the attached envelope.

_____ 4.   a.   Eliminate conscious bias, and concentrate on collecting accurate information when interviewing potential interns.
           b.   Discussing the proposal should be limited to 15 minutes; then, report the conclusions to Mr. Allred.
           c.   Please complete a financial report for April; and when you have reviewed the report, you should plan a board meeting to review the figures.

_____ 5.   a.   Matt's Equipment Inc. has designed a new printing machine, and the machine is engineered for simplicity of use.
           b.   User fees are being charged by foreign airlines, although similar fees are being considered by domestic carriers.
           c.   Business travelers are allowed reduced fares, but tour groups are usually provided the lowest fares.

_____ 6.   a.   The court recently ruled that police may detain an individual for 48 hours without a warrant. [The writer wants to make a statement of fact.]
           b.   In your new assignment, plan to devote about 60-70 percent of your time to working with clients. [The writer wants to give a command.]
           c.   Ms. Ostergar is concerned that she may have to give up her ambition to run for the Senate. [The writer wishes to express doubt.]

_____ 7.   a.   Jens Huszthy told me, "Take a deep breath before beginning a speech, and then you should just speak normally."
           b.   After retirement, Julius mowed and trimmed the lawn on Monday; but the rest of the week was devoted to fishing.
           c.   At one point during the hike, Tiffin literally ran to catch up; but she soon found herself unable to keep up the pace.

Correct all mood and voice errors. Two sentences contain no errors.

1. Most department employees are complimented for their accomplishments, which helps them to be motivated.

2. An internship is more vital than ever; you should seek a summer internship with Ernst and Young.

3. Will you please show Mr. Osguthorpe his new office in the Tanner Building. [imperative mood]

4. Ms. Brasher requested that Sherryl meet her at the Dallas airport. [subjunctive mood]

5. We appreciate the results of your consulting with Mr. Darais, and your name was suggested as a replacement for the city treasurer.

6. Space Age Technologies, Inc. has developed a clear, protective coating that will protect paint finish from acid-rain damage.

7. The conference will run three days; you should be allowed you to attend all the sessions.

8. Word process your stock report to make it look professional, and you should receive a good grade.

9. Would you request Janice to attend the regional conference as our representative. [A statement in the form of a polite directive is desired.]

10. Today, I would like to talk to you about budgeting.

11. Preregistration for the conference should begin June 10, so please watch for a brochure listing the procedures to follow.

Correct all mood and voice errors. Two sentences contain no errors.

1. We received the contractor's estimate, but our response has not yet been prepared.

2. If I was you, Andres, I would reconsider your decision to transfer to New Jersey.

3. Tell the superintendent to return the shipment via air freight, and then he can process a refund request.

4. Yes, we obtained the appropriate search warrant; but the results of the search have not yet been analyzed.

5. As I am sure you know, if I was going to play in the golf tournament, I would ask you to be my partner.

6. When the officer reported the accident, she stated that neither of the drivers was responsible for what happened.

7. Travel expenses would be tax deductible under the new law passed by Congress.

8. As we reviewed the impact of the study, several proposals were developed.

9. The consultant presented her conclusions as though she were experienced in international monetary policy.

10. Reporting the study findings should be limited to five minutes; then, take no more than ten minutes to discuss the recommendations.

11. Legal documents are signed only after thorough review and consultation. [Writer wishes to de-emphasize the object receiving the action.]

12. I have more confidence in what the taxpayer told me than in what I was told by his counsel.

MODIFIERS

DISCUSSION

If you like variety, you will appreciate the contribution modifiers make to good writing.

How important are modifiers? Try writing a sentence without them. You can do it, of course (*Money talks!* is an example). However, such sentences are infrequent. You will see few such sentences in a paragraph, a memo, a letter, or a report. For most good writing, we need *describing words* (modifiers) that help clarify or explain other key words we want to use.

The skillful writer uses modifiers effectively in nearly every sentence. Modifiers help us describe the subject of a sentence, the action that takes place, and the relationships between things and ideas.

However, just as the proper use of modifiers strengthens our writing, the careless use of these describing words weakens it. Writing can quickly become murky or ambiguous if modifiers are misused. The use of too many modifiers, misplaced modifiers, or the wrong modifiers results in poor writing. Learning to use modifiers properly will help you be an effective writer.

Modifiers are classified into two categories—**adjectives** (including clauses or phrases used as adjectives) and **adverbs** (including clauses or phrases used as adverbs).

Adjectives describe nouns and pronouns (*things*) and tell the reader what kind of *thing* and which *thing*. As describing words, adjectives make the meaning of nouns and pronouns as precise as possible.

Adverbs describe verbs (action words), adjectives, and other adverbs and answer such questions as *Where? When? How?* and *How much?* Like adjectives, adverbs are describing words that explain or clarify other words to give meaning and understanding to our language.

Modifiers (adjectives and adverbs) can be an asset to the writer who knows how to use them. They provide useful choices in communicating successfully with the reader. And they can make our writing interesting and precise.

Strengthen the quality of your writing by using modifiers properly when you write. The rules and learning tips that follow will help you.

TERMINOLOGY

Adjective—A word that describes a noun or a pronoun.

The briefcase is in the new office. (*The* and *new* are adjectives.)

Adverb—A word that describes a verb, an adjective, or another adverb.

Joan pronounced all particularly difficult words very distinctly. (*Particularly, very,* and *distinctly* are adverbs. *Particularly* describes *difficult,* an adjective; *very* describes *distinctly,* an adverb; and *distinctly* describes *pronounced,* a verb.)

Comparative degree—A comparison of two persons or things.

Don is **taller** than Ed.
Sue sang **better** today than she did yesterday.
Mr. Day is **less** demanding than we expected.

Compound modifier—Two or more words acting together as a single modifier.

Arnold is a well-behaved student who lives in a high-rise apartment. (Both *well-behaved* and *high-rise* are compound modifiers.)

Consecutive modifiers—Two or more modifiers in an uninterrupted series of modifiers that are unequal in rank and that are not, therefore, separated by commas.

tasty fruit cake
rustic log cabin

Coordinate compound modifier—A compound modifier that occurs in sequence with at least one other modifier of equal rank. Coordinate compound modifiers are separated by commas.

Lucinda is the young-looking, well-dressed executive in sales.
The project needs a hard-working, strong-minded leader.

Coordinate modifiers—Two or more modifiers that describe the same word; that are equal in rank; and that are, therefore, separated by commas.

happy, cheerful worker

long, detailed statement

Dangling modifier—A phrase stating an action or condition that does not logically and grammatically attach to the subject of the main clause of the sentence.

Shaking with emotion, a beautiful tribute was given by a close, personal friend. (*Shaking with emotion* is a dangling modifying phrase because it does not logically attach to *tribute*, the subject of the main clause of the sentence. The following improved construction eliminates the dangling modifier: *Shaking with emotion, a close, personal friend gave a beautiful tribute*.)

Misplaced modifier—A word, phrase, or clause (usually a phrase) that is not positioned properly with respect to the word or words it is meant to describe.

The picture is in your office that was bought at the auction. (*That was bought at the auction* is a misplaced modifying phrase because it illogically seems to refer to *office* rather than to *picture*.)

Incomplete comparison—A confusing or unclear statement resulting from failure to name both terms of a comparison.

I feel better today. (Better than what? Better than yesterday? Better than I expected to feel? Better than someone else?)

Modifier—A single word, a phrase, or a clause used to describe or define some element of a sentence.

sunny day (*sunny* is a single-word modifier)
Standing at the podium, Sarah spoke to the audience. (*Standing at the podium* is a modifying phrase.)
The man who left the message is Mr. Jenkins. (*Who left the message* is a dependent modifying clause.)

Positive degree—Reference to a characteristic or quality of one person or thing.

Don is **tall**.
Sue sang **well** today.

Proper adjective—A capitalized term that names a particular person, place, or thing and that functions as a modifier rather than as a noun.

Christmas Eve party
Bonneville Investment Company policies

Superlative degree—A comparison of three or more persons or things.

Don is the **tallest** boy in his class.

Sue is the **best** singer in the choir.

Compared to high taxes and high unemployment, moderate inflation is the **least** of three evils.

RULES

1. Place modifiers as closely as possible to the words they modify.

Pay attention to the simple matter of language geography when you write. By doing so, you can often avoid the confusion and ambiguity that result from misplaced modifiers.

NOT: The shipment was inspected by our warehouse manager that was received today.

BUT: The shipment received today was inspected by our warehouse manager.

ALSO: Our warehouse manager inspected the shipment received today.

Learning Tip 1: Place a single-word adjective immediately before the word it modifies.

NOT: An **old stack** of documents is on your desk.

BUT: A stack of **old documents** is on your desk

NOT: May I have a **cold glass** of water?

BUT: May I have a glass of **cold water**?

NOT: We need a **strong group** of voices for the choir.

BUT: We need a group of **strong voices** for the choir.

Learning Tip 2: A few adverbs (*actually, almost, also, just, merely, nearly, only,* and *quite*) are particularly troublesome. Place them as closely as possible to the words they modify. Notice how the meaning of the language changes depending on where the adverb is placed in the following sentences:

Jim can *only* attend the Thursday meetings. (Jim can't do anything but attend the meetings.)

Jim can attend the Thursday meetings *only*. (Of all the meetings scheduled, Jim can attend only those held on Thursday.)

NOT: I *almost* believe she is ready to graduate. (I don't quite believe it.)

BUT: I believe she is *almost* ready to graduate. (She will be ready to graduate soon.)

NOT: Claire plans to *also* write a letter. (Claire is going to do some other things in addition to writing.)

BUT: Claire *also* plans to write a letter. (Claire and someone else will write letters.)

Learning Tip 3:   Adverbs usually follow the words they modify. For emphasis, however, adverbs occasionally precede the words they modify. The choice of position should reflect the writer's good judgment and intent.

The fans cheered loudly for the team. (The adverb *loudly* is positioned in the customary place following the word it modifies.)

The fans loudly cheered for the team. (The writer emphasizes the adverb *loudly* by placing it before the word it modifies.)

---

2.   **Place a hyphen between the words of a compound modifier that precedes a noun. Hyphens are usually omitted in compound modifiers that follow a noun. (See Punctuation Rule 11.)**

Miyuke is a well-qualified manager.
As a manager, Miyuke is well qualified.

Send this memo to part-time workers.
Send this memo to employees who work part time.

Congratulations on a well-prepared and up-to-date resume.
Congratulations on a resume that is well prepared and up to date.

Learning Tip 4:   All self-word compounds are hyphenated whether they precede or follow a noun.

. . . self-protected software
. . . software that is self-protected

. . . self-serving comment
. . . a comment that is self-serving

She is a self-confident performer.
As a performer, she is self-confident.

Learning Tip 5: Compound modifiers that are multiple-word proper adjectives are **not** hyphenated except in rare instances.

The announcement was a General Manager directive.
All meetings were held on the Georgetown University campus.
Plans have been completed for this year's Super Bowl extravaganza.
The Coca-Cola Bottling Company is located at 825 South Freedom Boulevard.

General Manager, Georgetown University, Super Bowl, and *Coca-Cola* are all multiple-word proper adjectives. The Coca-Cola Company prefers to hyphenate the multiple-word proper adjective. Very few companies or organizations use a hyphen in multiple-word proper adjectives.

Please give me the name of a good German-American restaurant
The Bill-of-Rights solution is to protect the rights of individuals.
The Church of Jesus Christ of Latter-day Saints is headquartered in Salt Lake City.

The above three sentences illustrate multiple-word proper adjectives that are correctly hyphenated.

3. Distinguish between coordinate and consecutive modifiers, and punctuate them correctly. (See Punctuation Rule 10.)

Some adjectives that occur in a series of two or more words or terms before a noun do not form logical compound modifiers and are therefore not hyphenated. Such adjectives are either coordinate or consecutive, depending on whether they are equal in rank. Coordinate adjectives are separated by commas; consecutive adjectives are not.

Coordinate adjectives are equal in rank. Because they do not join logically together to form a compound modifier, they are not hyphenated. Instead, they are separated by commas.

NOT: Marty is a tall-skinny teenager.

BUT: Marty is a tall, skinny teenager.

NOT: Please order a bronze-fluorescent lamp for the office.

BUT: Please order a bronze, fluorescent lamp for the office.

Consecutive adjectives describe the same word but are unequal in rank. Like coordinate adjectives, they do not join logically together to form compound modifiers and are therefore not hyphenated. However, because they have unequal rank as describing words, they are **not** separated by commas. (Usually, the modifier closer to the word being described has the higher rank.)

NOT: You should wear a white-dress shirt.
             I need a dependable-executive assistant.

NOT: You should wear a white, dress shirt.
             I need a dependable, executive assistant.

BUT: You should wear a white dress shirt
             I need a dependable executive assistant.

Learning Tip 6: If you are uncertain whether to use a comma with a series of modifiers that do not function as a compound, try this test. Reverse the positions of the modifiers and insert the word *and* between them. If the meaning of the sentence remains unchanged and the language sounds natural, use a comma; otherwise, do not use a comma.

NOT: Stuart lives in a large, brick house. (Reversing *large* and *brick* and inserting *and* does not produce a natural sound. Therefore, a comma is not needed.)

BUT: Stuart lives in a large brick house.

NOT: Delilah has transferred to a modern progressive firm in Atlanta.

BUT: Delilah has transferred to a modern, progressive firm in Atlanta. (Reversing *modern* and *progressive* and inserting *and* produces a natural sound. Therefore, a comma is needed.)

---

4. Avoid dangling modifiers.

Modifying phrases that do not logically refer to a noun or a pronoun serving as the subject of the main clause of a sentence are said to "dangle." Dangling modifiers contribute to awkward language that confuses the reader.

Dangling modifiers usually (but not always) occur at the beginning of a main clause. Remember that the action spoken of in an introductory modifying phrase is attributed to the subject that follows.

Traveling at speeds above 80 miles per hour, the train derailed near Springdale.

Learning Tip 7: To recognize a dangling modifier, find the subject of the independent clause following the modifying phrase, put the subject in front of the modifying phrase, and then read the rest of the sentence. If the sentence is not logical when read in this order, you have a dangling modifier.

NOT: Snarling and foaming at the mouth, the dogcatcher had to restrain the rabid dog.

becomes

The dogcatcher, snarling and foaming at the mouth . . . .

BUT: Snarling and foaming at the mouth, the dog had to be restrained by the dogcatcher.

Learning Tip 8: One easy way to correct a dangling modifier is to change the subject of the main clause to a subject that is logically responsible for the action in the modifying phrase. The modifier thus can be given something logical to relate to. In addition, related words can be easily kept together.

NOT: To attend the meeting, a change in Carol's plans is required. (The "change" cannot attend the meeting.)

NOT: To attend the meeting, Carol's plans must be changed. (The "plans" cannot attend the meeting.)

BUT: To attend the meeting, Carol must change her plans. (Carol can attend the meeting.)

NOT: Leaving his office, the door was locked and the lights were turned off. (The "door" cannot leave the office.)

BUT: Leaving his office, Wayne locked the door and turned out the lights. (Wayne can leave the office.)

NOT: Noted for her writing ability, the seminar will be addressed by Professor Jane Addams. (The seminar is not noted for its writing ability.)

BUT: Noted for her writing ability, Professor Jane Addams will address the seminar. (Professor Addams is noted for her writing ability.)

Learning Tip 9: Another way to correct a dangling modifier at the beginning of a sentence is to change the modifying phrase to an introductory dependent clause with a subject of its own. Be careful, however, that you do not create a shift in voice with this procedure.

NOT: Knowing the deadline was approaching, the audit was quickly completed by the accountant. (The audit cannot "know" anything.)

NOT: Because the accountant knew the deadline was approaching, the audit was quickly completed. (The sentence contains a shift from active to passive voice.)

BUT: Because the accountant knew the deadline was approaching, she quickly completed the audit.

NOT: To avoid further delays, a final decision must be made immediately. (A decision cannot avoid delays; people avoid delays.)

NOT: If the committee wants to avoid further delays, a final decision must be made. (The sentence contains a shift from active to passive voice.)

BUT: If the committee wants to avoid further delays, it must make a final decision immediately.

Learning Tip 10: Dangling modifiers occasionally occur at the end of a sentence. In fact, novice writers often attempt to fix a front-of-sentence dangling modifier by moving the modifier to the end of the sentence. Whether at the front of a sentence or at the end of a sentence, modifying phrases that do not have a logical subject to modify are dangling modifiers. End-of-sentence dangling modifiers are corrected much like front-of-sentence dangling modifiers.

NOT: Stereotyped expressions should be avoided in choosing the words for your message.

BUT: Stereotyped expressions should be avoided when the words for your message are chosen.

ALSO: You should avoid stereotyped expressions in choosing the words for your message.

5. Use the correct form or degree of a modifier to make clear and logical comparisons.

Adjectives and adverbs are often used to compare things. The positive form of an adjective or an adverb is used to refer to a single characteristic. The comparative form is used to compare two things. The superlative form is used to compare three or more things.

The comparative form of an adjective results from the addition of *-er* to the positive form (*richer, poorer, older, faster*, etc.). Words such as *more* or *less* also are used in the comparative form (*more money, more people, less time, less efficient*, etc.).

NOT: He is the richest of those two businessmen.

BUT: He is the richer of those two businessmen.

NOT: Of the two speakers, Mr. Jones was the least nervous.

BUT: Of the two speakers, Mr. Jones was less nervous than Mr. Lee.

The superlative form indicates the greatest or least amount or degree of something. Adding *-est* to the positive form or using words such as *most* or *least* is characteristic of the superlative form.

NOT: Linda is the faster reader in the group.

BUT: Linda is the fastest reader in the group.

NOT: Rolphe is less likely to be late than our other employees.

BUT: Rolphe is the least likely of our employees to be late.

Learning Tip 11: Watch out for incomplete comparisons! When you compare two or more things, be sure to include in your language everything required to make the comparison clear and complete.

NOT: Daniel is a better writer this year. (Better than what?)

BUT: Daniel is a better writer this year than Lyle.

ALSO: Daniel is a better writer this year than he was last year.
         Daniel is a better writer this year than we expected him to be.

MODIFIERS

Daniel is the best writer in the class this year. (The superlative form is required here since Daniel is being compared with more than one other writer.)

Learning Tip 12: Avoid confusion when comparing someone or something in a group with other members of the same group. Use the words *other* or *else* to make such comparisons.

NOT: Renee is a better player than any member of her team. (Because Renee is one of the team members, this statement illogically says Renee is better than herself.)

BUT: Renee is the best player on her team.

ALSO: Renee is a better player than any other member of her team.
Renee is a better player than anyone else on her team.

NOT: Doug is less cooperative than anyone in his group. (As one of the people in his group, Doug cannot be less cooperative than himself.)

BUT: Doug is less cooperative than anyone else in his group.

ALSO: Doug is the least cooperative person in his group.

---

6. Avoid dropping the *-ly* ending from frequently used adverbs.

She sure is smart and *Drive careful going to school* are two often-used expressions. They are, however, grammatically incorrect. Correct usage for these statements is *She surely is smart* and *Drive carefully going to school*. In these examples, both *surely* and *carefully* are adverbs because they modify verbs; the *-ly* ending is therefore appropriate.

Remember that adverbs are used to describe verbs, adjectives, and other adverbs. Unfortunately, we often use—incorrectly—adjectives in place of adverbs by dropping the *-ly* ending from the adverb. Such errors are generally tolerated in day-to-day conversation, but we definitely should avoid them in our writing.

Many adverbs are formed when the *-ly* ending is added to an adjective. Note the following examples:

Adjective	Adverb
bad	badly
beautiful	beautifully

careful	carefully
honest	honestly
kind	kindly
real	really

Adjective	**Adverb**
scarce	scarcely
slow	slowly
sure	surely
sweet	sweetly
true	truly
willing	willingly

Being able to determine whether an adjective or an adverb is called for as a modifier helps the writer decide whether the *-ly* ending is appropriate.

NOT: We scarce could hear his voice on the telephone.

BUT: We scarcely could hear his voice on the telephone.

NOT: Speak slow enough to be understood.

BUT: Speak slowly enough to be understood.

NOT: When Darren called, Beulah answered very quick.

BUT: When Darren called, Beulah answered very quickly.

Learning Tip 13: Do not use a hyphen with adverb-adjective modifiers if the adverb ends in -ly. (See Punctuation Learning Tip 15.)

A well-written proposal
A carefully written proposal (no hyphen)

Those fresh-looking vegetables
Those freshly cooked vegetables (no hyphen)

Our always-late guests
Our habitually late guests (no hyphen)

MODIFIERS SELF-EVALUATION

Write *C* if the sentence is correct; write *I* if the sentence is incorrect. Compare your answers with those on the answer sheet. For each item you missed, review the explanation and, if necessary, study the material again.

_____ 1. The cargo was examined by the dock supervisor that was loaded this morning.

_____ 2. Daybreak was followed quietly by a spectacular sunrise.

_____ 3. Would you like a hot bowl of soup?

_____ 4. A customer is on the telephone with a complaint.

_____ 5. Marianne is younger than any contestant in the pageant.

_____ 6. In looking back, I can honestly say I am a wiser person.

_____ 7. John yelled loudly when his name was announced by the judges.

_____ 8. A black, leather book was found in the library reading room.

_____ 9. Dr. Troycer can only see patients on Tuesdays and Thursdays.

_____10. Although she is a self-confident speaker, she is not self confident as a writer.

_____11. Goldwaters is known as a decidedly upscale department store.

_____12. The interview led to a badly-needed job offer.

_____13. The Fosters hope to buy a small inexpensive house in the suburbs.

_____14. Begin slow with any new exercise program you decide to follow.

_____15. Hearing the clock strike twelve o'clock, the lunch break was taken by the office staff.

_____16. Of the two applicants, Rosemary is better prepared.

_____17. The Labor Day parade will be held on September 5 this year.

_____18. Old-fashioned clothes are gaining in popularity.

ANSWERS TO MODIFIERS SELF-EVALUATION

1. I   Place the modifying clause *that was loaded this morning* next to *cargo,* the word the modifying clause describes. (Rule 1)

2. C   The adverb *quietly* correctly follows the verb it modifies. (Rule 1; LT3)

3. I   Move the modifier *hot* closer to *soup,* the word *hot* describes. (Rule 1; LT1)

4. I   Place the phrase *with a complaint* closer to *customer,* the word it modifies. (Rule 1)

5. I   Use *other* in this comparison to avoid illogical, confusing language. (LT12)

6. I   Avoid incomplete comparisons. (Wiser than what? when? whom?) (Rule 5; LT11)

7. C   The *-ly* ending in *loudly* properly forms the appropriate adverb. (Rule 6; LT3)

8. C   The coordinate adjectives are properly separated by a comma. The comma is correctly omitted between the consecutive adjectives *library* and *reading.* (Rule 3; LT6)

9. I   Place the adverb *only* closer to *Tuesdays and Thursdays,* the words *only* modifies. (Rule 1; LT2)

10. I   All *self-* words are hyphenated whether they precede or follow a noun. (LT4)

11. C   The consecutive adjectives *upscale* and *department* are unequal in rank and are not separated by a comma. (LT13; Rule 3)

12. I   Do not hyphenate adverb-adjective modifiers if the adverb ends in *-ly.* (LT13)

13. I   Separate the coordinate adjectives *small* and *inexpensive* by a comma. (Rule 3; LT6)

14. I   Add the *-ly* ending to *slow* to form the appropriate adverb. (Rule 6)

15. I   The introductory modifying phrase is a dangling modifier that does not attach logically to *lunch break,* the subject of the main clause. (Rule 4)

16. C   The comparative form of the modifier is used to compare two people. (Rule 5)

17. C   Compound modifiers that are multiple-word proper adjectives are not hyphenated. (LT5)

18. C   The compound modifier *old-fashioned* precedes a noun and is correctly hyphenated. (Rule 2)

MODIFIERS EXERCISE 3   Name_____

Write *A* if the first choice in parentheses is correct; write *B* if the second choice is correct.

_____ 1. The patient decided to consult a second (well-regarded/well regarded) physician.

_____ 2. The (elderly-looking/elderly looking) man in the car is my uncle.

_____ 3. In terms of net profits thus far in this decade, 1993 is the (better/best) year.

_____ 4. The police officer hurried (quick/quickly) to the scene of the accident.

_____ 5. We believe the court (surely/sure) will impose a stiff sentence on the defendant.

_____ 6. We recently hired an (experienced, capable/experienced capable) sales manager.

_____ 7. David is a better worker than (anyone in his office/anyone else in his office).

_____ 8. The disappointing news caused the applicant to reply (angry/angrily).

_____ 9. Miss Tan selected Lori's puzzle as the (less/least) difficult of the four submitted.

_____10. We saw Mr. Waite driving a (rusty, dump truck/rusty dump truck) today.

_____11. The attorney, Jo Tada, is certainly (self-confident/well-qualified), don't you agree?

_____12. For your trouble, you will receive a (fresh box of chocolates/crystal-clear vase).

_____13. The firm's headquarters is located in a (heavily populated area/modern attractive building) in Denver.

_____14. Examining the report carefully, (the manager concluded it is accurate/it appeared to the manager to be accurate).

_____15. In reviewing our employees' records, (the conclusion was clear that Miss Noyes has the most seniority/we determined that Miss Noyes has the most seniority).

_____16. The school counselor is regarded as our (finest speaker on the faculty/first-choice for commencement speaker).

_____17. The publication titled (*Self Assured People in Business/Self-Assured People in Business*) is a witty, insightful treatment of a timely topic.

_____18. We were pleased to find a (well-dressed, pleasant-looking/well-dressed pleasant-looking) young woman at the reception desk.

MODIFIERS   113

MODIFIERS EXERCISE 4

Name_____

Write *AJ* if the bold word is an adjective; write *AV* if it is an adverb. Beginning with Item 11, two responses are required. Underline the subject of each clause once; underline the verb or verb phrase of each clause twice; and then bracket each dependent clause.

_____ 1. I plan to approach the assigned task **enthusiastically**.

_____ 2. A **careful** reading of the will produced a major surprise.

_____ 3. The teacher rebuked the **noisy** student kindly but firmly.

_____ 4. Mona expects to earn a **higher** salary this year than Reba.

_____ 5. A substantial salary increase, however, is **truly** out of the question.

_____ 6. The runner crossed the finish line in the **fastest** time of the year.

_____ 7. When Marvin jumped **higher** than he had ever jumped before, he surprised himself as well as his teammates.

_____ 8. Following months of tedious practice, Doreen gave a **very** impressive performance on opening night.

_____ 9. She believed she had played **badly** until the judges declared her the winner.

_____10. Attitude and behavior in the face of adversity are the **real** measures of a person's character.

_____11. A **significant** evaluation of the Keystone Project will be undertaken **promptly** when Mr. Koche returns to Columbus.

_____12. The **revised** projections are **almost** ready for review by the finance committee.

_____13. According to Frank, we **just** may get the wage increases we have worked so **hard** to obtain.

_____14. The architect will not quite finish the **needed** specifications by the deadline; I am **quite** certain of that.

_____15. **Only** three people applied for the job, and all three applicants are **largely** unqualified for the position.

_____16. Mr. Thomas' new snow thrower has a **quick**-start feature that works well in **cold** weather.

Write the letter identifying the sentence that uses modifiers correctly.

____1.   a.   Louisa said she is fascinated by your interesting, factual report.
         b.   Ms. Wilson's seminar was reported to be well-organized, insightful, and professionally conducted.
         c.   Only two of our seven finalists were properly-dressed for the contest.

____2.   a.   Do your work very careful to achieve a successful outcome.
         b.   Drive as slow as good judgment dictates is prudent to avoid injury.
         c.   Dawn received your message and is surely grateful for your support.

____3.   a.   My experience with Kim suggests she is a self-starter.
         b.   May we use your new Dutch-oven to cook a tasty meal for our boys?
         c.   Paul can only hope his application to be a fireman will be accepted by the city personnel office.

____4.   a.   We are pleased the results of the exam are substantially higher this year.
         b.   My role in the project is smaller than Harvey's.
         c.   Lloyd's experience and qualifications are much stronger than Neil, according to the interviewer.

____5.   a.   The manager will announce the names of only those who exceed their assigned sales quota.
         b.   We need a person to oversee the staff with strong leadership skills.
         c.   A complaint was received by our office that was written by M. L. Blant.

____6.   a.   The laser printer makes easy to read, good looking documents.
         b.   At 5 p.m., please take the boxes to the small, mail room.
         c.   Speak kindly to the person who was especially careful with our packages.

____7.   a.   After leaving home at age 18, I worked for a large life-insurance firm.
         b.   I always believed that a strong performance on a smaller job leads to opportunities for a bigger job.
         c.   Before getting my recent promotion, Kay interviewed me at great length.

____8.   a.   Compared to your first letter, the second one is the best.
         b.   To answer your simple, direct query, I suggest an adjustable, durable chair.
         c.   You need a strong bottle of cough syrup for that nagging cold.

____9.   a.   The new supervisor is self-confident and well-organized.
         b.   Run fast and yell loud if you need help.
         c.   I am less qualified than you, but Toby is the least qualified of all of us.

Write the letter identifying **each** sentence that uses modifiers correctly. Some items require more than one answer.

_____1.   a.   I can't quite arrive at work as early as you can.
            b.   The Starlight Restaurant features a fresh menu of meat and fish.
            c.   Were you the only one to earn a perfect score on the quiz?

_____2.   a.   May I see your high school diploma?
            b.   The nicest feature of the *Tribune* is its use of large, bold type.
            c.   Does delicious, warm apple pie for dessert appeal to you?

_____3.   a.   A thorough self-examination of one's personality can be revealing.
            b.   This year's New Year's Day football games are intriguing, to say the least.
            c.   You will be able to recognize me by my purple, baseball cap.

_____4.   a.   The comedienne opened with a humorous entertaining monologue.
            b.   To be sure you understand, the instructions will be repeated slowly.
            c.   Of all the people who applied, only Tony Spandos was more nervous after the interview than before.

_____5.   a.   Is Teresa rather than Millicent the newest auditor in our group?
            b.   After hearing your story, I honestly don't know what to believe.
            c.   Compared to the other days of the week, Monday is the least busy in our office.

_____6.   a.   A genuinely-deserved compliment should be readily given.
            b.   A rebuke—even if richly deserved—should be expressed only reluctantly.
            c.   A sincere, tastefully-stated commendation is rarely out of place.

_____7.   a.   Please stop at the self-service, automatic car wash on your way to work.
            b.   The biggest shopping day of the year comes immediately after the Thanksgiving Day holiday.
            c.   A convenient and inexpensive photo touch-up service is offered by Modern Photographers at the Apple Tree Road location.

_____8.   a.   Anticipating a change in the weather, our reasons for going camping were challenged by Ms. Kong.
            b.   A series of large, clearly marked signs is now in place on Interstate 80.
            c.   I believe your proposal is best—despite Mr. Fritter's objections—than any of the others submitted.

_____9.   a.   Which of the triplets in your family is slower in losing her temper?
            b.   Has the walk-up window been a true convenience for those who use it?
            c.   Self-protected files must meet new requirements for self-protection in the future.

Edit the following sentences to correct all errors in the use of modifiers. Two of the sentences contain no errors.

1. Please answer the white cordless telephone on the desk in the study.

2. You will see the population sign as you approach the Mill-City outskirts.

3. A stylish, wool sweater can be purchased at Snooter's for a surprisingly-low cost of $25.

4. As you will see on his application, no other candidate possesses better qualifications.

5. Growling angrily, the huge grizzly bear was finally quieted by the young animal trainer.

6. Parking his car at the curb, Walter approached the small dimly-lit doorway.

7. The surprised frightened boy—startled by the explosion—ran quick out the door.

8. Who is less likely to be uncooperative—Hans, Gretel, or Bubba?

9. If the teacher agrees to raise Lorna's grade in advanced-writing, we sure will be surprised.

10. A well educated person is not necessarily qualified to be an interesting stimulating speaker.

11. No one in the seventh grade has a better attendance record than Juanita Reyes.

12. The teacher entered the classroom carrying a large, briefcase bulging with test-papers.

13. As a mechanic in our service-department, Hal is both competent and self sufficient.

14. As a well-trained, computer specialist, we should hire Carla immediately.

Edit the following sentences to correct all errors in the use of modifiers. Two of the sentences contain no errors.

1. Fresh, tasty fruitcake and tangy eggnog are among my favorite Christmas treats.

2. Speaking for our group, the financial analysis project assigned to us seems overly-difficult.

3. Even though you are the younger of three daughters, you must set a high suitably modest standard of personal conduct.

4. The new quaintly decorated office was assigned to Ms. Ladd, our senior, sales executive.

5. As the newer student in class, we want Carlos to be well-received from the very first day.

6. The newly, revised recipe calls for 1 pint of premium, whipping cream and 2 fresh cups of strawberries.

7. All first time, Idaho-Oil customers are fully-eligible candidates for the grand prize award.

8. A delicious box of cashew nut candy will be gladly given to each early arriving fan.

9. Heavy darkening clouds threatened the afternoon, baseball game as well as several other carefully-planned events.

10. After examining the brief, newspaper article carefully, the reporter self confidently expressed a surprising point-of-view.

11. The least amount of money Jorge can make during the current calendar year is much more than he reportedly made last year.

12. The well prepared manager opened the main doors at 8-a.m. sharp to a long, grumpy line of impatient customers.

CONNECTIVES

DISCUSSION

Good writing requires words, phrases, and clauses to be joined in certain ways. The words and punctuation marks that join these sentence parts are called *connectives*. Properly used, connectives give clarity, consistency, and correct form to our writing.

In the English language, connectives function as signals. The brake lights and turn signals on an automobile are used to indicate the car is going to stop, slow down, or change direction. Similarly, connectives tell the reader whether to expect a continuation of a particular thought, the addition of a similar thought, or the introduction of a new thought.

In addition to joining sentence parts—words, phrases, and clauses—connectives also show relationships between ideas. This function—showing relationships—is called coordination and subordination. In showing such relationships, connectives foster *parallelism* (consistency) in the grammatical structure of a sentence and in the way ideas are expressed.

Parallel language is logical in form and meaning. It "feels" comfortable to the reader, and it is easier to understand than language that is not parallel. Parallelism is an essential element in clear and effective communication, and connectives are vital components in achieving this important language quality.

Often-used connectives include *coordinating conjunctions, correlative conjunctions, conjunctive adverbs, subordinating conjunctions, relative pronouns, prepositions,* and certain punctuation marks. Most connectives are words with which you are already familiar.

By using connectives correctly, you will achieve parallelism in your writing—the proper connecting, coordinating, and subordinating of sentence parts and ideas. You will thus increase the probability your writing will achieve the desired result.

An understanding of what connectives are and how to use them is essential to the effective writer. Study the rules and learning tips carefully in this chapter to further improve your writing skills.

Conjunctive adverb—A connective adverb such as *therefore* or *however* that joins independent clauses to each other and that shows relationships between the clauses.

Your work is finished; *therefore*, you may go home.

I plan to attend the dinner; *however*, I cannot remain for the program to follow.

Connective—A word or punctuation mark that joins sentence parts to each other. Connectives frequently show relationships between the parts and provide desired emphasis in our writing. Conjunctions and prepositions are the most-important connectives.

Chicago and Los Angeles are major U.S. cities; one of them is my home town. (The conjunction *and*, the preposition *of*, and the semicolon are all connectives.)

Coordinating conjunction—A connective word such as *and, but*, or *yet* that joins sentence elements of equal grammatical importance—words with words, phrases with phrases, clauses with clauses.

Registration will be held today and tomorrow. (Equal words are joined by the coordinating conjunction *and*.)

The play opened to a large room but to a small audience. (Equal phrases are joined by the coordinating conjunction *but*.)

Michael attended the meeting, yet he was unable to talk to Mr. Zenkert. (Equal clauses are joined by the coordinating conjunction *yet*.)

Correlative conjunctions (connected pair)—Conjunctions used in pairs (i.e., *not only . . . but also; neither . . . nor*) to join words, phrases, and clauses that are grammatically equal in rank. (Pronounce the word *correlative* **core-el-a-tiv**.)

The movie is *not only* interesting *but also* educational.

According to the receptionist, *neither* Mr. Wiley *nor* Ms. Clatter is available.

Dependent (subordinate) clause—A group of related words that does not present a complete thought but instead depends on some word in the independent clause of the same sentence to complete its meaning.

As you know, the semester ends Friday. (*As you know* is a dependent clause.)

Nancy is the student who received the highest grade in the class. (*Who received the highest grade in the class* is a dependent clause.)

Double prepositions—Two prepositions that needlessly occur next to each other.

When the plane gets *up in* the air, we can focus *in on* the problem.

Essential (restrictive) clause—A clause that is essential to the meaning of the sentence. Essential clauses are not set off with punctuation.

The personnel file *that Mr. Sample requested* is on your desk.

The customer *who left the message* is Mrs. Wardelle.

Independent (main) clause—A group of related words that can stand alone as a complete thought or statement.

The office opens at 8 a.m.

As indicated by the survey, all the workers are high-school graduates. (*All the workers are high-school graduates* is an independent clause.)

Nonessential (nonrestrictive) clause—A clause that is not essential to the meaning of the sentence. Nonessential clauses are set off in the sentence—usually with commas.

The monthly newsletter, *which you will find interesting*, is in your box.

Mandee Powers, *who is the editor of the newsletter*, has announced her retirement.

Parallelism—The expression of two or more ideas of equal importance in coordinate or consistent grammatical form (words joined to words, phrases joined to phrases, clauses joined to clauses).

Dick *and* Jane; sooner *or* later (words joined to words)

In the morning *or* in the afternoon; a long day's work *and* a good night's sleep (phrases joined to phrases)

Parley is here now, *but* Jerald will come later. (independent clause joined to independent clause)

Phrasal preposition—Two or more words that act together as one preposition.

in regard to   in the event that
for the purpose of

Preposition—A connective word such as *at, of, on, over, about, above, with,* etc., used to join the word, phrase, or clause that follows it to some other element in the sentence.

The firm announced **on** Wednesday that employees **over** age 55 **with** 20 years **or** more **of** service may qualify **for** early retirement. (All words in bold print are prepositions.)

Prepositional phrase—A group of words consisting of a preposition, its object, and any words that modify the object.

in the morning
after the ball game
before the September 30 deadline

Relative pronoun—A connective pronoun such as *that, who,* or *which* functioning as a conjunction in the dependent clause it introduces and connecting the dependent clause to the rest of the sentence.

The car *that* was stolen is mine.

The reporter *who* spoke to our writing class works for the *Mt. Pilot Sentinel*.

We now know *which* candidate will be elected governor.

Split construction—A sentence structure that splits or divides closely related sentence elements and that requires different prepositions to complete two or more related words.

Mary Beth is interested *in* and prepared *for* a course in advanced calculus.

The probation officer has an understanding *of* and experience *with* juvenile delinquency.

Subordinating conjunction—A word such as *although, unless, after,* or *before* that limits—or subordinates—the clause it introduces, resulting in an incomplete thought that depends on a main clause for complete meaning.

After Deke went home, he worked in the garden.

Deke will work in the garden again tomorrow *unless he is too tired*.

Terminal preposition—A preposition that occurs at the end of a sentence. (Usually—but not always—terminal prepositions should be avoided.)

This map shows where my house is *at*.

What page are you reading *on*?

You will be interested to know where Peter got this quotation *from*.

RULES

> **1.** Use a coordinating conjunction (*and, but, or, for, nor, so,* and *yet*) to join two independent clauses or other sentence elements of equal rank. (See Punctuation Rule 1.)

Coordinate means *parallel* or *equal*. A coordinating conjunction is used to join clauses, phrases, and words that are parallel—equal in rank or importance. In the following examples, note the use of coordinating conjunctions to join parallel clauses, phrases, and words. Remember that a clause contains both a subject and a verb; a phrase does not.

Ruth is playing hard, and her team is doing well. (parallel—or equal—clauses joined by the coordinating conjunction *and*)

The supervisor did not attend the meeting, yet he required all of us to be there. (parallel clauses joined by the coordinating conjunction *yet*)

Deedee is expecting a letter from Mrs. Tooler or from Ms. Pointy. (parallel phrases joined by the coordinating conjunction *or*)

"Difficult but fair" is Anne's impression of the final examination. (parallel words joined by the coordinating conjunction *but*)

Learning Tip 1: Insert a comma before a coordinating conjunction that joins two independent clauses. (See Punctuation Rule 1.)

NOT: Write a check for $50 and mail it no later than noon.

BUT: Write a check for $50, and mail it no later than noon.

Learning Tip 2: To avoid comma confusion, insert a semicolon before a coordinating conjunction that joins two independent clauses if commas occur elsewhere in either of the independent clauses. (See Punctuation Rule 1, Learning Tip 5.)

NOT: According to Mary, the bill has been paid, but the latest statement indicates no payment was received.

BUT: According to Mary, the bill has been paid; but the latest statement indicates no payment was received.

Learning Tip 3: A conjunction may be used occasionally at the beginning of a sentence as a signal to emphasize direction. Use such beginnings sparingly, however, to avoid weak, choppy writing.

NOT: The pool is well lighted. And it is conveniently located. But it is poorly maintained. And it has inadequate parking for patrons.

BUT: The pool is well lighted and conveniently located. But the park is poorly maintained and has inadequate parking for patrons.

---

2. Use conjunctive adverbs to join independent clauses, to show relationships between the clauses, and to signal emphasis or direction. Most conjunctive adverbs (such as *therefore, however, accordingly, nonetheless, furthermore, consequently,* and *unfortunately*) are multiple-syllable words. Four common, one-syllable conjunctive adverbs are *still, hence, then,* and *thus.* (See Punctuation Rule 3.)

NOT: The contract was signed immediately by both parties. Actual construction will not begin for at least 90 days.

BUT: The contract was signed immediately by both parties; *however,* actual construction will not begin for at least 90 days.

NOT: The contractor missed the construction deadline; the workmanship failed to meet the architect's specifications.

BUT: The contractor missed the construction deadline; *furthermore,* the workmanship failed to meet the architect's specifications.

Learning Tip 4: Transitional phrases such as *in fact, in the meantime, for example, in addition, in other words, on the other hand,* and *as a matter of fact* function as conjunctive adverbs in joining two independent clauses.

Give careful thought to the proposal to be submitted in June; *in the meantime,* review last year's proposal thoroughly.

The textbook for the accounting course is new; *in fact,* the textbook has not yet arrived at the bookstore.

Learning Tip 5: Place a semicolon immediately before and a comma immediately after a conjunctive adverb or transitional phrase.

> The meeting of the planning committee has been postponed; *accordingly,* our trip to Baltimore must be rescheduled.

> Della is a particularly thoughtful secretary; *for example,* she always remembers her coworkers on their birthdays.

---

3. **Use a semicolon to join independent clauses that are closely related in meaning but that are *not* connected by a coordinating conjunction or by a conjunctive adverb. (See Punctuation Rule 2.)**

Some punctuation marks—the semicolon, the comma, the dash, and the colon—are used to join sentence elements. The semicolon is especially useful in joining independent clauses that are closely related in meaning. In certain instances, therefore, the semicolon is used in place of words to join sentence parts.

> The proposal is nearly complete; the final draft is expected this afternoon.

> Mr. Dawes will arrive on Flight 330; Juan will meet him at the airport.

Learning Tip 6: The semicolon—not the comma—is sometimes used without words to connect closely related independent clauses. If a comma only is used to connect two independent clauses, the result is an unwanted comma splice.

> **NOT:** The office desk you requested costs $675, a less-expensive desk is being considered.

> **BUT:** The office desk you requested costs $675; a less-expensive desk is being considered.

---

4. **Use relative pronouns (*that, who, whom, which, whoever, whomever, whichever* and *whatever*) to show subordination of dependent clauses.**

Relative pronouns are frequently used to indicate subordination of dependent clauses and to join the clauses they introduce to the rest of the sentence.

> The appointment *that* was made yesterday was canceled today.

> The oil shipment, *which* we discussed Thursday, has arrived at Pier 9.

CONNECTIVES

A reporter *who* works for the *Daily Herald* is waiting in your office.

I will gladly speak to *whomever* you suggest.

Learning Tip 7: Choose correctly between *that* and *which* when using one of these two words to introduce a dependent clause. *That* is used to introduce a restrictive clause (one that is essential to the meaning of the sentence). *Which* is used to introduce a nonrestrictive clause (one that is **not** essential to the meaning of the sentence).

Restrictive clauses need no special punctuation; nonrestrictive clauses are usually set off with commas.

> The car that you see in the driveway is mine. (The restrictive clause *that you see in the driveway* is essential to the meaning of the sentence.)

> Mr. Simmons' latest order, which arrived by mail this morning, has been misplaced. (The nonrestrictive clause *which arrived by mail this morning* is not essential to the meaning of the sentence and is set off with commas.)

Learning Tip 8: Be consistent and logical in using relative pronouns to join two or more related sentence elements.

> **NOT:** The report *that* was prepared yesterday and *which* you received this morning should be read immediately.

> **BUT:** The report *that* was prepared yesterday and *that* you received this morning should be read immediately.

> **NOT:** The announcement, *which* was dated March 31 and *that* was unexpected, contained nothing new.

> **BUT:** The announcement, *which* was dated March 31 and *which* was unexpected, contained nothing new.

Learning Tip 9: Use *who* or *whom* to refer to a person. Use *that* or *which* to refer to a thing.

> **NOT:** The girl *that* was hired is new in town.

> **BUT:** The girl *who* was hired is new in town.

> **NOT:** The satisfied customer, *which* you met this morning, sent us a thank-you note.

BUT:	The satisfied customer, *whom* you met this morning, sent us a thank-you note.
NOT:	The Dalton Company, *who* is one of our best customers, has opened an office in Yuma.
BUT:	The Dalton Company, *which* is one of our best customers, has opened an office in Yuma.
ALSO:	The firm *that* is our best customer—The Dalton Company—has opened an office in Yuma.

5. Use correctly the words *when*, *where*, and *while* to introduce subordinate clauses.

In using *when, where,* and *while,* remember these important distinctions: *when* indicates a fixed or stated period of time or a specific point in time; *where* relates to place or location; and *while* refers to a duration of time.

The Christmas season is *when* air travel is most intense.
When Chris arrives with your order, pay him from the petty-cash account.

New York is *where* the Statue of Liberty is located.
I plan to live *where* sunshine is plentiful.

Judy printed the charts on the photocopier *while* Tonya collated and stapled the brochure.
While the school assembly was in progress, a small fire began in the media center.

Learning Tip 10: Avoid using *when* and *where* to give definitions.

NOT:	Access in writing is *when* you use white space to give variety to printed text.
BUT:	Access in writing is using white space to give variety to printed text.
NOT:	A comma splice is *where* two independent clauses are joined only by a comma.
BUT:	A comma splice is the use of only a comma to join two independent clauses.

Also, avoid using *while* to show contrast or comparison. Instead, show contrast or comparison through the use of such words as *although, though, whereas,* or *but.*

CONNECTIVES

NOT:	*While* your suggestion was helpful, it did not solve the problem entirely.
BUT:	Although your suggestion was helpful, it did not solve the problem entirely.

6. Use subordinating conjunctions to join unequal sentence elements (such as an independent clause and a dependent clause). (See Punctuation Rules 4 and 5.)

Some conjunctions are used to limit—or subordinate—the sentence elements they introduce. These subordinated elements often are clauses that are not complete thoughts and, therefore, cannot stand alone. For complete meaning, they depend on a main clause elsewhere in the same sentence.

Following are a few examples of familiar and frequently used subordinating conjunctions:

after	before	so that	where
although	if	unless	whereas
as	inasmuch as	until	while
because	provided	when	whether

All student records must be reviewed and updated *before* school begins.

Your hotel accommodations are definitely guaranteed *inasmuch as* your reservation was confirmed.

The demonstration continued near the entrance to the building *while* the meeting was in progress.

The order was not received until after Christmas, *although* the order was shipped on December 10.

Learning Tip 11: A comma is used to set off a dependent clause or an introductory phrase that precedes an independent clause. On the other hand, a dependent clause that follows an independent clause usually is not set off by commas unless the dependent clause is nonrestrictive.

NOT:	Classes will begin Tuesday because Labor Day is celebrated on Monday. (The dependent clause *because Labor Day is celebrated on Monday* is **restrictive**—essential to the meaning of the sentence—and should not be set off by a comma.)
BUT:	Classes will begin on Tuesday rather than Monday, although we expected an earlier start. (The dependent clause *although we expected an earlier*

start is **nonrestrictive**—not essential to the meaning of the sentence—and should be set off by a comma.)

Whether a clause is restrictive or nonrestrictive often must be determined by your best judgment. Determining whether the clause in question is essential to the intended meaning of the sentence will be an important factor in your decision.

---

7. Use correlative conjunctions (connected pairs) to connect sentence elements—words, phrases, clauses—that are parallel (grammatically equal).

Correlative conjunctions are always used as pairs. They are useful joiners if a sentence contains two or more grammatically equal elements. You will have occasion to use the following correlative conjunctions in your writing:

either . . . or	whether . . . or
neither . . . nor	since . . . therefore
if . . . then	not only . . . but also
both . . . and	

If our offer is accepted, *then* we will buy the house on Lakeside Avenue.

Our proposal was *not only* approved *but also* admired for its originality and design.

Learning Tip 12. To assure correct grammatical form, avoid using only one member of a correlative pair. Also, make sure both members of the correlative pair are followed by the same part of speech or by the same grammatical construction.

NOT: Jake's monograph not only uses charts but photographs. (Only one member of the correlative pair *not only . . . but also* is used.)

NOT: Jake's monograph not only uses charts but also photographs. (Not only is followed by a verb; *but also* is followed by a noun.)

BUT: Jake's monograph uses not only charts but also photographs. (Both members of the correlative pair *not only . . . but also* are used, and both are followed by a noun.)

NOT: The company is considering whether to hire more workers or get by with our present staff. (*Whether* is followed by an infinitive phrase; *or* is followed by a verb.)

BUT: The company is considering whether to hire more workers or to get by with our present staff. (Both *whether* and *or* are followed by an infinitive phrase.)

Learning Tip 13: Avoid mixing the first half of one connective pair with the second half of another pair.

NOT: *Either* the foreman *nor* the crew chief can explain the slowdown.

BUT: *Neither* the foreman *nor* the crew chief can explain the slowdown.

NOT: We understand that *both* the title *but also* the abstract are in the County Assessor's Office.

BUT: We understand that *both* the title *and* the abstract are in the County Assessor's Office.

---

8. Use simple prepositions and short, simple words rather than wordy phrasal constructions as connectives.

Good writing is clear and concise. Wordy expressions interfere with effective communication. Choose simple prepositions and other short, simple terms over multiple-word phrasal constructions.

Choose	Rather than
about, concerning	in regard to
after	subsequent to
because	due to the fact that
before	prior to
to	for the purpose of
if	in the event that
to	in order to

NOT: *Subsequent to* Mr. Tischner's arrival, a meeting was held for the entire staff.

BUT: *After* Mr. Tischner's arrival, a meeting was held for the entire staff.

NOT: *Due to the fact that* I was out of the office, I did not get your call.

BUT: *Because* I was out of the office, I did not get your call.

Double prepositions and useless end-of-sentence terminal prepositions are examples of using prepositions needlessly. Wordiness and awkward expressions result when prepositions are used to excess.

NOT: When can you start *in on* the manuscript?

BUT: When can you start the manuscript.

NOT: Do you know where the Johnson file is *at*?

BUT: Do you know where the Johnson file is?

Learning Tip 14: You may have heard that a preposition should not be placed at the end of a sentence. In general, that's true. In some cases, however, exceptions are made. Most writers consider terminal prepositions acceptable if such prepositions contribute to the clarity and "comfortableness" of the language.

Note the use of end-of-sentence prepositions to achieve clear and natural expression.

I wish I knew where this note came from.

How much inconvenience are you willing to put up with?

What sorority does Jannelle belong to?

Which airline are you going to fly on?

Some terminal prepositions are awkward and serve no useful purpose. They definitely should be avoided.

NOT: Where did Warren park his car at?

BUT: Where did Warren park his car?

NOT: You are welcome to try this calculator out.

BUT: You are welcome to try this calculator.

In general, avoid ending a sentence with a preposition. Make an exception, however, when terminal prepositions improve the clarity and naturalness of your writing.

Ideas of equal importance should have parallel grammatical structure. Therefore, repeat the preposition before the second of two parallel ideas.

NOT: Joni wants to visit our office and meet our staff.

BUT: Joni wants *to* visit our office and *to* meet our staff.

NOT: Our auditors excel by following sound procedures and demanding high standards.

BUT: Our auditors excel *by* following sound procedures and *by* demanding high standards.

A split construction in a sentence requires different prepositions to complete the meaning of two or more words. If only one preposition is used when two or more prepositions are needed, an awkward expression results. Use a **logical** preposition for **each** word to be completed in a split construction.

NOT: Mason has an aptitude and a background in quantum physics.

BUT: Mason has *an aptitude for* and *a background in* quantum physics.

NOT: Melissa will enroll and graduate from Chapman College.

BUT: Melissa will *enroll in* and *graduate from* Chapman College.

The prize money should be divided equally *between* Sam and Torrey
Who *among* the three of us has the most computer experience?

NOT: The competition was keen *between* the three top contestants.

BUT: The competition was keen *among* the three top contestants.

NOT: Please divide your attention *among* Sallee Torson and Jana Koyle.

BUT: Please divide your attention *between* Sallee Torson and Jana Koyle.

CONNECTIVES SELF-EVALUATION

Write *C* if the sentence is correct; write *I* if the sentence is incorrect. Compare your answers with those on the answer sheet. For each item you miss, review the explanation and, if necessary, study the material again.

_____ 1. Traffic is heavy today and accidents are likely to occur.

_____ 2. If you can attend the seminar in Memphis, yet the experience should be genuinely valuable.

_____ 3. Mrs. Doone, the receptionist, is in the office, but she will not be there long.

_____ 4. Jim is well trained for his job; in fact, he is the best-qualified manager in the company.

_____ 5. Geraldine informed us that the police officer whom you spoke to this morning is Rhonda Konrad.

_____ 6. Dr. Willardson was present while the operation was being performed.

_____ 7. In the event that you don't agree to our conditions, please contact us immediately.

_____ 8. Professor Loppey expects to complete her research and report the results at the November conference.

_____ 9. An argument erupted between the three angry members of the city council concerning the proposed tax increase.

_____ 10. Every pledge made during the fund-raising drive was paid; furthermore, less money was collected than expected.

_____ 11. Assembly-line output is at an all-time high in the Minneapolis plant, we couldn't be more pleased.

_____ 12. Will you please describe the research project that is now underway in our Portland lab?

_____ 13. The student who came to your office and that inquired about graduation requirements will return tomorrow.

_____ 14. A late assignment is when the student gives the teacher an exercise after the date the assignment is due.

ANSWERS TO CONNECTIVES SELF-EVALUATION

1. I   Insert a comma before the coordinating conjunction *and* that joins two independent clauses. (LT1)

2. I   The coordinating conjunction *yet* is incorrectly used to join two clauses that are unequal in rank. (Rule 1)

3. I   Avoid comma confusion by inserting a semicolon before a coordinating conjunction that joins two independent clauses if commas occur elsewhere in either of the independent clauses. (LT2)

4. C   The transitional phrase *in fact* is correctly used to join two independent clauses. Also, the transitional phrase is properly punctuated with a semicolon before and a comma after the phrase. (LT4; LT5)

5. C   The relative pronoun *whom* is correctly used to refer to a person. (LT9)

6. C   The word *while* is correctly used to indicate a duration of time. (Rule 5)

7. I   The simple preposition *if* should be used in place of the wordy phrasal construction *in the event that*. (Rule 8)

8. I   The preposition *to* should be repeated before the second parallel idea expressed in the sentence. The correct construction should read . . . *to complete her research and to report the results* . . . (Rule 10)

9. I   The preposition *among* should be used to refer to more than two people. (Rule 11)

10. I   The use of the conjunctive adverb *furthermore* to connect the two independent clauses in this sentence suggests an illogical relationship between the clauses. *Nevertheless, however,* or *nonetheless* is a better choice. (Rule 2)

11. I   The incorrect use of only a comma to join independent clauses results in a comma splice. In this instance, a semicolon is an appropriate choice because the clauses are closely related in meaning. (LT6)

12. C   The relative pronoun *that* is correctly used to introduce the restrictive clause *that is now underway in our Portland lab.* (LT7)

13. I   The relative pronoun *who* should be used consistently in both instances to refer to a person. (LT9)

14. I   The word *when* is incorrectly used to give a definition. (LT10)

CONNECTIVES EXERCISE 1   Name_____

Write *T* if the statement is true; write *F* if the statement is false.

_____ 1.   A prepositional phrase and a phrasal preposition are the same thing.

_____ 2.   A clause contains a subject and a verb; a phrase does not.

_____ 3.   *But, for, yet,* and *nor* are all examples of coordinating conjunctions.

_____ 4.   A conjunction should never be used at the beginning of a sentence.

_____ 5.   Transitional phrases—when they are used as connectives—function in the same way
           as conjunctive adverbs.

_____ 6.   If a semicolon is used to join two independent clauses, the semicolon must be
           accompanied by a coordinating conjunction such as *and* or *but*.

_____ 7.   The words *when, where,* and *what* are all used to introduce subordinate clauses.

_____ 8.   The words *when* and *while* both may be used to give a definition.

_____ 9.   *Although, until,* and *because* are examples of conjunctions that limit or subordinate the
           sentence elements they introduce.

_____10.   *Correlative conjunctions* and *connected pairs* refer to the same thing.

_____11.   The simple preposition *before* should be used in place of the wordy phrasal
           construction *in the event that*.

_____12.   *Due to the fact that Bob was out of town, the meeting was canceled* illustrates the use
           of a wordy phrasal construction.

_____13.   *Do you know where Jason is transferring to?* illustrates an undesirable terminal
           preposition.

_____14.   Some terminal prepositions are undesirable; some are not.

_____15.   *Lolita has cooking experience with and a passion for Chinese food* illustrates a
           correctly expressed split construction.

_____16.   The preposition *between* is used to refer only to people; the preposition *among* is used
           to refer only to things.

CONNECTIVES EXERCISE 2   Name_____

Write *C* to indicate the sentence is correct; write *I* to indicate the sentence is incorrect. Underline the subject of each clause once; underline the verb or verb phrase of each clause twice; and then bracket each dependent clause.

_____ 1.   Prior to the January 21 meeting, all overdue charges had been paid in full.

_____ 2.   The article reported that both Seattle or Boise are being considered as the host city.

_____ 3.   The final interviews will be conducted while Mr. Bussey is in Washington, D.C.

_____ 4.   The bridge will open to traffic on Thanksgiving Day; the mayor will cut the ribbon.

_____ 5.   A compound sentence is when a sentence contains at least two independent clauses.

_____ 6.   I will be glad to see you on Thursday or Friday, whichever day is more convenient.

_____ 7.   The final examination is on Tuesday but course grades will not be announced until later.

_____ 8.   Ms. Tuckle, the supervisor, as well as Tamara, you, and I will work on the project; but my role will be advisory only.

_____ 9.   The contract contains a missed-deadline penalty, however, bad weather may justify an exception.

_____10.   The play's opening scene, that is very short, introduces all the main characters.

_____11.   The abstract was written by Lanny Kingster who also wrote the preface to the article.

_____12.   Harry Marke will be transferred to the Denver office unless he decides to retire early.

_____13.   The firm expects not only to show a profit this quarter but also to strengthen its position in the international market.

_____14.   Shirley, please take this package up to Ms. Carney's office on the ninth floor.

_____15.   Barbara plans to visit the zoo and take Cassandra with her.

_____16.   The ill will that exists between Ray, Darryl, and their supervisor must be eliminated immediately.

_____17.   Unfortunately, the personnel officer, Ms. Krunck, nor the recruiting supervisor, Andrea Kohler, will be able to visit our campus this spring.

CONNECTIVES EXERCISE 5   Name_____

Write the letter of the statement that uses connectives correctly.

____1.   a.   The proposal is ready for review, and George will begin the review process.
       b.   The review process is lengthy; however the results justify the time and effort.
       c.   We expect the results to be successful, but, we won't know until March 10.

____2.   a.   The firm shows negative growth this year, yet conditions will improve soon.
       b.   Exports will rise sharply next year and imports will follow suit.
       c.   High profits are expected in the coming year, nonetheless stiff competition will come from abroad.

____3.   a.   The two options are still being debated by the board, we will be informed when a decision is made.
       b.   Miss McGill canceled the appointment, furthermore, she will schedule another appointment soon.
       c.   As announced, Roger, Frank, and Jane have been transferred to Sales; Frank, however, is the only one of the three to receive a raise.

____4.   a.   A geological survey team is in place; and, Craig Webb is acting as team leader.
       b.   Travel arrangements for the surveyors are complete; their departure date is September 30.
       c.   The survey team's first stop is St. Louis; accordingly the St. Louis office is making plans for the team's arrival.

____5.   a.   The budget preview will be presented in Room 480, questions concerning the budget are invited.
       b.   The budget preview, that occurs each November, is essential to good planning.
       c.   Next year's budget committee chairperson, who will be announced next month, is expected to be a CPA from the accounting section.

____6.   a.   Dolly Rayes or Markie Poler, whichever you select, will be asked to serve on the activities committee.
       b.   The doctor that we talked to this morning and issued the prescription for Bifferall is a specialist in blood diseases.
       c.   The AKP Company is a firm that will do a lot of business with us in the future.

____7.   a.   The road crew is working overtime, whereas our crew has too little work to do.
       b.   Overstaffing is when a firm has too many employees for the work to be done.
       c.   Offices will be closed Monday, because of the Independence Day holiday.

____8.   a.   Neither the student from Chicago and the salesman from Detroit will get the job.
       b.   The bill is due today; however, we will be able to make only a partial payment.
       c.   The cause of the fire which occurred in the downtown area is still unknown.

CONNECTIVES EXERCISE 6   Name_____

Write the letter identifying **each** sentence that uses connectives correctly. Some items require more than one answer.

_____1. a. You should know that not only Rhoda in Purchasing or Wilma in Receiving is eligible for the Excellent Employee Award.
         b. Due to the fact that the project is new, it does not yet have a name.
         c. Either the sales representative in Billings or the division supervisor in Tucson will be this year's performance leader.

_____2. a. We will meet at 4 p.m. up in Sophie Turkle's tenth-floor office.
         b. May I speak to you concerning the hospital charges for the Trina Liau injury?
         c. From which university did Cora Bukowski get her degree?

_____3. a. At which restaurant does the boss usually eat lunch at?
         b. We intend to interview everyone and then to suggest a new slogan.
         c. All visitors to the museum must enter in at Portal 3.

_____4. a. Somewhere among the six candidates is Ohio's next U.S. senator.
         b. Loretta is interested in but confused by Zaki's conflicting explanations.
         c. Have you decided whether the Michigan shopping mall or the Oregon housing project will be undertaken next?

_____5. a. All cities where our branch offices are located will be visited by the CEO.
         b. The city which will be visited first is Knoxville.
         c. The Knoxville manager, whom the CEO greatly admires, is one of the company's most-progressive executives.

_____6. a. We intend to honor Noelle Brown at tonight's game, for she has the highest batting average in the league.
         b. Noelle's flight arrives at 3:30, so you must be at the airport no later than 2:45.
         c. Take Noelle directly to the Hotel Ritz; in addition, arrange transportation for her to the stadium this evening.

_____7. a. We hope to see you in San Francisco; but our travel schedule is still uncertain.
         b. The building inspector, whom you criticized, has been transferred.
         c. Neither of the two canceled checks which you requested recently but which are missing from our files has been located.

_____8. a. The crew will eat dinner at the Red Fox Diner, after the day's work is done.
         b. If you can't accept our invitation, please call me immediately.
         c. The dispute among the four judges was prompted by the keen competition between the two finalists.

Edit the following sentences to correct all errors in the use of connectives. Two of the sentences contain no errors.

1. Post the announcement on the bulletin board, send a copy to the *Morning Sentinel*.

2. The early-morning shift, that includes over 400 workers, begins promptly at 6 a.m.

3. We know that if enough employees sign up, then we will qualify for reduced rates.

4. Arthur must choose between Harvard, Yale, and Princeton before the March 15 deadline.

5. The maintenance technician is down in the basement servicing the furnace.

6. Our attorney plans to file an appeal and develop a new legal strategy for another trial.

7. The dedication will take place at the site where the battle was fought in 1863.

8. All companies who are interested in the project are invited to submit bids which meet the requirements specified by the architect.

9. Tom has worked his way up from an entry-level job to the position which he now occupies.

10. A fight broke out among the two candidates; nevertheless the debates were successful.

11. While you start up the computer, check the E-mail and make copies of all messages.

12. Although Frances is one of our newest sales representatives in the Southwest Division; she is the leader in gross sales volume this year.

13. None of the managers which we recruited for the Pacific Zone has a background or an aptitude for personnel management.

Edit the following sentences to correct all errors in the use of connectives. Two of the sentences contain no errors.

1. Out of the five companies which submitted bids, only two are from the western states.

2. The choice is between Miami and Key West; nevertheless, neither is favored over the other.

3. Bill lives in Genoa while Bob lives in Claxton; but, both Bob and Bill plan to move soon.

4. The train wreck which occurred near Wilmington is being investigated by the Department of Transportation, that has jurisdiction in such matters.

5. Two orientation meetings must be attended by all new employees, a third meeting, that was proposed over a year ago, may be added to the schedule.

6. The ceremony will be at noon, nevertheless; neither Harold or Bill will attend.

7. Shellie is the city official that requested a change in plans. Accordingly, the date was changed.

8. Where do you suppose the machinery which we urgently need was shipped to?

9. The revised production schedule, which you told us about only yesterday and which we will have difficulty meeting, should be reconsidered by whoever devised it.

10. While our business is growing by leaps and bounds, the quality of our service is not keeping pace. Nonetheless, we must make every effort to improve.

11. After completing the estimates, take them to Accounting who is located on the eighth floor.

12. We haven't heard whether Mr. Samsel or Mr. Daiglee is the investigator that will not only inspect the warehouse nor make recommendations for necessary modifications.

PUNCTUATION

DISCUSSION

Punctuation helps make sentence content clear to your reader. Proper punctuation helps your reader understand the sentence-part relationships you want to convey. On the other hand, poor punctuation makes an unfavorable impression, causes confusion, and often forces the reader to reread the sentence.

About a hundred rules of punctuation can be identified. In the business world, about one-fourth of that number account for over 95 percent of all the punctuation used.

The implication of that fact is you can master the frequently used punctuation rules and know you are punctuating correctly about 90 percent of the time.

However, among the most frequently used punctuation rules are several that do not cause miscommunication if they are used incorrectly. For example, the colon following the salutation in a business letter does not necessarily result in better communication.

Our approach to punctuation reflects two thrusts:

1. Identify those punctuation rules that reflect frequently used punctuation practices in most disciplines.

2. Emphasize the punctuation rules that contribute significantly to communication effectiveness.

Through good punctuation reflecting those two thrusts, you can *intentionally* influence your readers to help them understand your message. That is, you can be totally consistent in your application of punctuation; force pauses at appropriate points; increase or decrease the amount of emphasis; clarify your meanings; give variety to your writing; and signal changes in direction or thought.

The rules that follow are critical to effective written communication. You can apply them consistently, and they will assure your using correct punctuation about 90 percent of the time.

TERMINOLOGY

Appositive—A noun or a noun phrase that identifies or explains its equivalent in the sentence.

> Ms. McMurtrie, our newly hired accountant, will call you tomorrow. (*Our newly hired accountant* is in apposition to *Ms. McMurtrie*.)
>
> Our newly hired accountant, Ms. McMurtrie, will call you tomorrow. (*Ms. McMurtrie* is in apposition to *our newly hired accountant*.)

Cadence test—A device used to determine what the noun is in multiple-word expressions and to determine whether any hyphens should be used in compound modifiers. The cadence test requires dramatic pauses between words in all possible combinations in a multiple-word expression. For example, does *bigger than life test case* contain a compound modifier?

> bigger   *than life test case*
> bigger-than   *life test case*
> bigger-than-life   *test case*
> bigger-than-life-test   *case*

Obviously, the pause between *bigger-than-life* and *test case* proves the noun is *test case* and the compound modifier is *bigger-than-life*.

Compound sentence—A sentence containing two or more independent clauses and no dependent clauses.

> I like the looks of your new car, and I want to buy one just like it.
> The car has the right price tag; however, I cannot afford a new car this year.

Clause—A "group of words" with both a subject and a verb.

> Stop! (The subject of the clause is *you*. The resulting clause is a sentence.)
> Freddy laughed at my joke. (The clause is an independent clause because it can "stand alone" as a sentence.)
> When you want me to speak, ... (The clause is a dependent clause because it cannot "stand alone" as a sentence; for meaning, the dependent clause "depends" on the independent clause that follows.)

Comma splice—A sentence containing two independent clauses joined with a comma only.

> I have my reasons for missing class, you must also have your reasons.
> We have scheduled your speech for 10 a.m., I hope your plane gets here in time.

Complex sentence—A sentence containing one independent clause and at least one dependent clause.

When you get to the meeting, Tom wants you to visit our display booth.
I learned a great deal in the course, although my grade seems to indicate otherwise.

Compound adjective—See *compound modifier*.

Compound modifier—Two or more hyphenated words that jointly modify a noun. Most compound modifiers are adjectives and, as such, are called *compound adjectives*. Adverb-adjective modifiers are often hyphenated if the adverb does not end in *-ly*. The procedures to test for compound modifiers are explained in Learning Tip 14.

fair-trade price
eighth-grade education
well-intentioned person

Conjunctive adverb—An adverb used to connect the independent clauses of a compound sentence. In such instances, a semicolon precedes and a comma follows the conjunctive adverb.

We have finished the project; *therefore*, we can go home for Thanksgiving.
Bill stated the policies precisely; *thus*, you have little reason for complaint.

Coordinate modifiers—Two or more parallel adjectives that describe the same noun; that are equal in rank; and that are separated by commas.

Ms. Kearl is an *intelligent, educated* person.
Barbra gave a *brief, interesting* summary of your presentation.

Coordinating conjunction—Any one of seven conjunctions (*and, but, or, for, nor, so, yet*) used to join independent clauses in a compound sentence.

I heard your presentation in Santa Fe, *and* I want you to give it in Los Alamos.
We have not sent in our room reservations, *nor* have we confirmed our flight schedule.
We attended the Kansas City conference, *but* we did not participate on the program.

Dependent clause—A group of words that contains a subject and a verb but that cannot stand alone—that is, a dependent clause is not a sentence. Also called a *subordinate clause*. A dependent clause usually begins with a subordinating conjunction.

Although we want the bid, ...
When you get to Orlando, ...
. . . that you hired a new person.

Fragment—A group of words that is an incomplete statement and that is punctuated as a complete sentence.

>Whereas Ms. Marshall favors the December 12 deadline.
>Anticipating the role he will play in introducing the new product.

Independent clause—A group of words that can stand alone—it can be a simple sentence. Also called a *main clause*.

>Jeffrey laughed.
>Take Benjamin with you.
>We want to spend the July 4 holiday at Lake Powell.

Nonessential modifier—A word, phrase, or clause that adds descriptive information but that could theoretically be omitted without changing the meaning. Also called a *nonrestrictive modifier*.

>My latest car, *which I bought from my uncle*, has been completely restored.
>Our student newspaper, *one of the best in the state*, won three awards.

Phrase—A group of words without a subject and a verb. Typically used as a noun, an adjective, or an adverb.

>*In the meantime*, Marvin decided to attend the conference.
>*Struggling to reach the top*, the climber slipped on the slick rocks.
>*To get the results*, return the postage-paid card within ten days.

Run-on sentence—A sentence containing two independent clauses but containing no punctuation or conjunctive joiner to connect the two clauses.

>My wife spent a month in France she returned to winter weather in St. Paul.
>The students wanted to sublet the apartment the landlord did not seem to object.

Sentence interrupter—A word or phrase occurring in the middle of a sentence to achieve transition between thoughts. Such words and phrases are used to show addition, comparison, contrast, results, summary, or time.

>I cannot attend the meetings, *however*, because of prior commitments.
>The final decision is, *as you suspected*, up to Mr. Gates.

Series—A plural noun describing a group of coordinate elements (items of the same grammatical construction) coming one after the other in succession. A series requires three or more items that are preferably joined/separated by commas. A conjunction is used between the last two items.

Plan to give the results of your study to Ms. Tada, to Mr. Sumsion, and to Ms. Winston.

For the trip, you will be wise to take your swimming suit, a beach towel, a large umbrella, and lots of sunscreen.

Subordinate clause—See *dependent clause*.

RULES

> **1. In a compound sentence, use a comma between two independent clauses joined by a coordinating conjunction. (See Connectives Rule 1.)**

We use the following seven coordinating conjunctions in English: *and, but, or, for, nor, so,* and *yet*. They are called *coordinating conjunctions* because they are used to connect grammatically equal (or coordinate) sentence elements. Notice that all seven coordinating conjunctions are one-syllable words.

NOT: The test measures a person's ability to adapt and we hope to administer it to all prospective employees.

BUT: The test measures a person's ability to adapt, and we hope to administer it to all prospective employees.

Learning Tip 1: Technically, the comma may be omitted if both the independent clauses are short—five or fewer words. For example:

Their order arrived yesterday and we shipped it today.
Pay attention in class or drop the course immediately.

For consistency reasons, all exercises in *Practical Grammar Review* require either a comma or a semicolon before a conjunction that joins two independent clauses.

Learning Tip 2: A comma by itself **cannot** be used to join two independent clauses. This practice results in a *comma splice* (the writer tries to join or "splice" the two independent clauses with a comma only). The comma splice is usually viewed as a "red flag of illiteracy." For example:

The supervisor has confidence in them, she encourages them to do their best at all times.

To correct a comma splice, revise the sentence in one of the ways discussed in Rules 1-3. The easiest method of correcting a comma splice is to replace the comma with a semicolon as directed in Rule 2.

Learning Tip 3: If independent clauses in a compound sentence are not joined through one of the directives in Rules 1-3, a *run-on sentence* results. The run-on sentence is usually viewed as a "red flag of illiteracy." For example:

> We expect to start with a flexible phone system we hope to add to it as our company expands.

To correct a run-on sentence, revise it in one of the ways discussed in Rules 1-3. The easiest correction is to place a semicolon between the independent clauses as suggested in Rule 2.

Learning Tip 4: The comma between independent clauses joined by a conjunction *may* be replaced with a semicolon. For example:

> We expect to start with a flexible phone system; and we hope to add to it as our company expands.

In the above example, note that a comma is *not* used following the conjunction *and*. If a comma were used following the conjunction in the above example, the writer would be confusing Rule 1 with Rule 3.

Learning Tip 5: If either of the independent clauses contains one or more commas that might result in *comma confusion*, a semicolon may replace the comma between the independent clauses.

NOT:	The first, second, and third sales meetings, according to Mr. Jones, will be held soon, but our director, Ms. Henson, will not be able to attend.
BUT:	The first, second, and third sales meetings, according to Mr. Jones, will be held soon; but our director, Ms. Henson, will not be able to attend.

All exercises in *Practical Grammar Review* require a semicolon before the conjunction in a compound sentence if either clause has one or more internal commas.

Learning Tip 6: Avoid inserting a comma or a semicolon before a conjunction that joins a compound verb. For example:

NOT:	The printer worked fine yesterday, and appeared to be working when I arrived this morning.

BUT:	The printer worked fine yesterday and appeared to be working when I arrived this morning.
OR:	The printer worked fine yesterday, and it appeared to be working when I arrived this morning.

Novice writers frequently place a comma before an *and*. In general, remember a comma precedes *and* in only two instances—when the *and* joins two independent clauses (Rule 1) or when the *and* joins items in a series (Rule 6).

---

2. In a compound sentence, use a semicolon between independent clauses that are not joined by a coordinating conjunction. (See Connectives Rule 3.)

Novice writers occasionally write sentences containing comma splices or run-on sentences. The easiest way to correct a comma splice or a run-on sentence is to join the two independent clauses with a semicolon. Notice the abrupt pause the semicolon demands between independent clauses.

NOT:	The meeting will be held soon, we expect to accomplish great things in the meeting. (This sentence contains a *comma splice*.)
NOT:	The meeting will be held soon we expect to accomplish great things in the meeting. (This sentence is a *run-on sentence*.)
BUT:	The meeting will be held soon; we expect to accomplish great things in the meeting.

In nearly every instance, the semicolon is used only when an independent clause both precedes it and follows it. Therefore, be wary of using a semicolon unless you are joining two or more independent clauses.

---

3. Use a semicolon before and a comma after a conjunctive adverb or a transitional phrase that joins two independent clauses. (See Connectives Rule 2.)

Most conjunctive adverbs are multiple-syllable words—for example, *moreover, however, consequently, subsequently*, and *therefore*. Four one-syllable conjunctive adverbs are *still, hence, then*, and *thus*.

NOT:	I cannot attend the meeting, nevertheless, you should try to resolve the major issues. (This sentence contains a *comma splice*.)

NOT:	I cannot attend the meeting; nevertheless you should try to resolve the major issues.
BUT:	I cannot attend the meeting; nevertheless, you should try to resolve the major issues.

Note the distinctions among coordinating conjunctions (Rule 1), subordinating conjunctions (Rule 4), and conjunctive adverbs (Rule 3). And note that a semicolon precedes a conjunctive adverb when the conjunctive adverb connects two independent clauses but not when the same word is used as a sentence interrupter (Rule 8).

---

4. Use a comma to set off a dependent clause that precedes an independent clause. (See Connectives Rule 6.)

A dependent clause is also called a subordinate clause because it *depends on* or is *subordinate to* the independent clause. Most dependent clauses begin with a *subordinating conjunction*, which subordinates the information in the dependent clause to the information in the independent clause. Typical subordinating conjunctions are *if, when, while, because, since, as, though, although, before, until*, and *unless*. By itself, a dependent clause is not a sentence but is a fragment if written as a sentence.

NOT:	As you can see the job requires considerable skill.
	If his work is satisfactory we will hire him.
	Because you want the vice president to give the keynote address.

BUT:	As you can see, the job requires considerable skill.
	If his work is satisfactory, we will hire him.
	Because you want the vice president to give the keynote address, we have moved Mr. Willoughby to an afternoon time.

Learning Tip 7: We form most dependent clauses by placing subordinating conjunctions in front of what otherwise would be independent clauses. For example, the following are independent clauses (each is a sentence):

You can see.
You have completed the assignment.
His work is satisfactory.
You prepared the work on time.

Notice how subordinating conjunctions change those independent clauses into dependent clauses (the clauses are no longer sentences):

As you can see, ...

When you have completed the assignment, ...
If his work is satisfactory, ...
Although you prepared the work on time, ...

5. Use a comma to set off a dependent clause that follows an independent clause if an obvious pause is desirable. (See Connectives Learning Tip 11.)

Very seldom do we set off a dependent clause with a comma when the clause follows an independent clause. However, if we want to give additional emphasis to the content of the dependent clause, we can set the clause off for emphasis. However, a dash is generally preferable to a comma for that purpose, as explained in Rule 9.

On the other hand, we do set off most dependent clauses that follow independent clauses if certain subordinating conjunctions are used to begin the dependent clauses. Those subordinating conjunctions are *as, whereas, though, even though*, and *although*.

NOT:	Most union members agreed to return to work although many of them did not like the contract's terms.
BUT:	Most union members agreed to return to work, although many of them did not like the contract's terms.
NOT:	We must have the stationery by April 1 as we must mail our form letter on April 5.
BUT:	We must have the stationery by April 1, as we must mail our form letter on April 5.

6. Use commas to separate words, phrases, or clauses in a series.

NOT:	The report contained tables, charts and graphs.
	The report can be found on top of my desk, in the middle file cabinet or among the papers in the outer office.
	The supervisor responded to such items as who provided the figures, why they were provided and who resolved the problems.
BUT:	The report contained tables, charts, and graphs.
	The report can be found on top of my desk, in the middle file cabinet, or among the papers in the outer office.
	The supervisor responded to such items as who provided the figures, why they were provided, and who resolved the problems.

PUNCTUATION

Learning Tip 8: A *series* involves three or more items arranged in sequence. If only two items are involved, the sentence does not contain a series; and the comma is incorrect.

    NOT: The report contained tables, and charts.
                The report can be found on top of my desk, or in the middle file cabinet.

    BUT: The report contained tables and charts.
                The report can be found on top of my desk or in the middle file cabinet.

Learning Tip 9: Novice writers frequently use a comma preceding nearly all conjunctions. For example:

The company declared a lower dividend than normal, but promised to replace the outdated equipment.

Such writers probably confuse Rule 1 (use commas before conjunctions in independent clauses) and Rule 6 (use commas to separate items in a series). Be watchful you do not succumb to a "comma-conjunction mentality."

Learning Tip 10: Some disciplines (such as journalism) suggest that the comma immediately preceding the conjunction in a series be eliminated. Although this practice does not cause confusion in most instances, it does in some.

In other disciplines (such as business), the comma immediately preceding the conjunction in a series is universally used. If you observe the rule consistently as stated, you will not write sentences that cause items-in-a-series comma confusion. Throughout *Practical Grammar Review*, we always require a comma before the conjunction in a series.

7. Use a comma to set off introductory words and phrases.

Single, nonessential words that precede independent clauses are used to achieve transition, to give emphasis, or to show a particular attitude toward the meaning being conveyed.

Through such words, the writer can show addition (*also, besides, furthermore*); consequence (*accordingly, otherwise, therefore, thus*); concession (*anyway, however, nevertheless*); or sequence (*afterward, finally, first, next*).

Or the writer can accomplish other objectives—such as reflect endorsement (*indeed*); show mild support (*apparently, presumably*); arouse emotion (*unfortunately, truthfully*); assume an honest position (*frankly, actually*); or reflect confirmation or disconfirmation (*yes, no*).

> *Incidentally*, we have sent your summary to the home office.
> *Ideally*, we should hold the sales conference in San Jose.
> *No*, I do not agree with Paula's assessment of the situation.

A phrase is a group of words without a subject or a verb. As pointed out in Rule 4, an introductory dependent clause is always set off with a comma. In a similar fashion, we recommend that **all** introductory phrases be set off with commas.

> *Between now and next month*, you should plan to expand the orientation seminar.
> *Hoping for the best*, we placed our first order.
> *To purchase the unit*, we completed the requisition today.
> We received our order six months after we placed it; *after complaining about the delay*, we received only a minor apology from your shipping department.

---

8. Use commas to set off internal sentence interrupters and to set off appositives.

The term *sentence interrupter* aptly describes three sentence elements that are set off with commas when the elements occur in the middle of a sentence. The three elements are nonessential modifiers, transitional elements, and parenthetical statements.

A nonessential modifier (also called a *nonrestrictive modifier*) is a dependent clause or phrase that does not limit or define the term it modifies. Theoretically, if the modifier were omitted, the meaning of the sentence would not change much.

> Many of the people we contacted, *who have lived in poverty for centuries*, desperately need our financial assistance.
> The report, *which I have read carefully*, is satisfactory.

Which clauses are almost always nonessential—they should be set off with commas. On the other hand, *that clauses* are essential and are never set off with commas.

Transitional elements are words or phrases used to achieve transition between thoughts. As explained in Rule 7, such items are set off with commas when they come at the first of a sentence. In a similar fashion, transitional elements are set off when they occur in the middle of a sentence—unless they are performing as conjunctive adverbs to join independent clauses as explained in Rule 3.

> The decision was, *nevertheless*, made in favor of my client.
> We have many reasons, *however*, to support the new proposal.

Parenthetical statements distinctively reflect the idea of an interrupter. We call such sentence elements parenthetical because they are qualifying or explanatory statements that could be put inside parentheses.

PUNCTUATION   153

The answer is, *as you can imagine*, very unpopular with us.
The supervisor, *hoping for the best*, gave the report to me.

An appositive is a noun or noun equivalent placed beside another noun as an explanatory equivalent. An appositive has much the same "feel" as a sentence interrupter. An appositive in the middle of a sentence is set off by commas; an appositive at the end of a sentence is preceded by a comma.

Mr. Henrie, *the committee chairperson*, was contacted today.
The assignment went to Kristine, *the new supervisor*.

Essential (restrictive) appositives are not set off with commas. For example:

My son Andrew recently graduated. (The writer has more than one son.)

---

9.   Use the dash to give emphasis or to show a sudden change in the structure of a sentence.

A dash forces a reader to pause dramatically. As such, the dash is the best punctuation mark to use when the writer wants to give emphasis to the material that follows the dash. If any criticism can be directed toward novice writers in relation to the dash, it is they probably tend to use it too infrequently. In business writing, the dash is a particularly useful punctuation mark.

Three workers—Ms. French, Mrs. Lee, and Mr. Church—were commended.
We will ask Mr. Williams—who is the only person we trust—how the plan was
    devised.
Only one member—the chairman—could account for the loss!
The result is as he predicted—as hard as we worked, we were not able to get the
    job done on time!
His decision is obvious—we will have to recall all the parts.
His attire is inappropriate—namely, his jacket and his shoes are not coordinated.

Learning Tip 11: In most of the sentences that illustrate Rule 9—especially those containing nonessential modifiers or parenthetical statements—commas, parentheses, or dashes may be used. However, dashes give more emphasis than either commas or parentheses.

Novice writers tend to avoid the dash. Your writing will improve if you consciously use the dash—especially to emphasize something.

Learning Tip 12: The dash is very effective in appending a *fragment* to the independent clause. For example:

NOT: The mistakes were "red-flag" illiteracy errors. Run-on sentences, comma splices, and dangling modifiers.

BUT: The mistakes were "red-flag" illiteracy errors—run-on sentences, comma splices, and dangling modifiers.

---

10. Use a comma to separate coordinate, parallel adjectives that precede a noun. (See Modifiers Rule 3.)

The term *coordinate* signals that the adjectives in a coordinate-adjective construction are equal to each other in content meaning and in grammatical construction.

Wesley completed the lengthy, detailed report this morning.
John performed his duties in a capable, conscientious way.

Learning Tip 13: Two ways to determine whether two adjectives should be separated by a comma are as follows:

1. Insert the word *and* between the adjectives. If the expression still reads smoothly with *and* inserted, the comma is correct.

2. Reverse the order of the adjectives. If the expression still reads smoothly and makes sense, the comma is correct.

For example:

Each salesperson will get an appropriate living allowance.

We cannot think sensibly of the allowance as being appropriate *and* living. Nor can we call the allowance a *living, appropriate allowance.* Therefore, no comma is needed to separate the consecutive adjectives.

---

11. Use a hyphen to join a compound modifier that precedes a noun. (See Modifiers Rule 2.)

Two or more words acting together as a single modifier before a noun are called a *compound modifier.*

Charley is definitely a *middle-class* American.
Monica does not consider herself a *career-driven* manager.
By December 31, our office will have *up-to-date* equipment.

I was dismayed at the *I'm-out-to-get-you* attitude.

Learning Tip 14: You will be successful in hyphenating compound modifiers if you can identify the noun in a multiple-word expression.

Nouns may consist of one word only or of two or more words without hyphens. For example, the following multiple-word terms are nouns without hyphens:

> gross national product
> conflict of interest
> condensed balance sheet
> cost of goods sold

In a similar respect, nouns that follow compound modifiers can be one word or more than one word. For example:

> fair-trade *price*
> carry-forward *working papers*
> indefinite-life *intangible fixed asset*
> full-paid *capital stock*

How do we determine the noun in relation to the modifiers in such expressions? One technique that works well in most instances is called the **cadence test**.

To use the cadence test, simply put a dramatic pause between the various options in a multiple-word expression. When your ear tells you the pause is a natural one, more than likely you will then know what the noun is and, therefore, what the compound modifier is.

For example, apply the cadence test as you read the following options out loud. Give a lengthy pause where indicated, and then decide whether the italicized expression following the pause is a normal one. In each instance, you're trying to determine whether the italicized item following the pause is the noun.

> full   *faith and credit debit*
> full-faith   *and credit debit*
> full-faith-and   *credit debit*
> full-faith-and-credit   *debit*

Obviously, the cadence test tells you Item 4 is the logical choice. Therefore, you know that *debit* is the noun and that hyphens must appear in the compound modifier: *full-faith-and-credit* debit.

Learning Tip 15: Most compound expressions are adjectives. Sometimes, however, the first word in a compound modifier is an adverb. Typically, if the adverb does not end in -*ly*, we place a hyphen between the adverb and the adjective. (See Modifiers Learning Tip 13.) In situations that involve an adverb ending in -*ly* plus an adjective, the hyphen is not used. For example:

NOT: He submitted a *well prepared* report to the committee.
            He submitted a *carefully-prepared* report to the committee.

BUT: He submitted a *well-prepared* report to the committee.
            He submitted a *carefully prepared* report to the committee.

Learning Tip 16: The hyphen is not used if the compound expression follows the noun. For example:

Precedes Noun	Follows Noun
up-to-date figures	The figures are *up to date*.
on-the-job training	We give training *on the job*.
change-of-address form	Please send me a form for a *change of address*.
door-to-door sales	Have you gone *door to door* to make sales?
ten-year-old student	The student is *ten years old*.
well-thought-out plan	The plan is *well thought out*.

Learning Tip 17: Today, nearly all compound words are formed without hyphens between the prefix and the word—whether the compounds are verbs, adjectives, or adverbs. When in doubt about whether to hyphenate a prefix, consult a recent, reputable dictionary. Some common, nonhyphenated prefixes are the following:

ante	anteroom	*post*	postdoctoral
anti	anticlerical	*pre*	preempt
co	coauthor	*re*	reexamine
inter	interrelated	*semi*	semicircular
intra	intrastate	*sub*	substandard
non	nonmember	*super*	supertanker
over	overeager	*un*	unfunded

> **12. Use a colon to emphasize the content relationship between independent clauses and to introduce statements, quotations, or lists.**

A colon can be used to join two independent clauses—much like the semicolon or the dash. In such instances, however, the colon emphasizes the **content** relationship between the independent clauses:

Your role on the committee is critical: you will have the tie-breaking vote in several instances.

Although writers may choose among the semicolon, dash, or colon to join independent clauses, most writers typically prefer the semicolon or the dash:

Your role on the committee is critical; you will have the tie-breaking vote in several instances.

Your role on the committee is critical—you will have the tie-breaking vote in several instances.

A colon is frequently used to introduce statements, quotations, or lists:

The policy will be stated thus: Use a personal vehicle only if a company vehicle is not available.

I quote Dr. Harold Smith: "In an educational sense, self-motivation is the difference between being on the defensive and being on the offensive."

Please bring the following items to the meeting: minutes of the last meeting, budget requests for the new year, and a schedule of activities for the new year.

Do not use a colon to introduce a sentence element that is the complement or object of an element in the introductory statement:

NOT: The four basic styles of leadership are: tells, sells, consults, and joins.

BUT: The four basic styles of leadership are tells, sells, consults, and joins.

Expressions such as *thus, that is, as follows,* or *the following* are typically used to introduce statements, quotations, or lists:

The four basic styles of leadership are as follows: tells, sells, consults, and joins.

PUNCTUATION SELF-EVALUATION

Write *C* if the sentence is correct; write *I* if the sentence is incorrect. Compare your answers with those on the answer sheet. For each item you missed, review the explanation and, if necessary, study the material again.

_____ 1. Use an outline to give your speech an effective beginning, middle, and ending.

_____ 2. Marketing courses must be taught in a business environment and instructors must have a business background to teach the courses properly.

_____ 3. Effective annual reports are written in clear simple language.

_____ 4. You should realize that accurate proofreading skills are essential to writing success; therefore, you should master effective editing rules and skills early in the course.

_____ 5. Many job descriptions—especially descriptions of new positions—are not up to date.

_____ 6. On the other hand Beth has extensive auditing experience.

_____ 7. Please submit the above mentioned forms in duplicate.

_____ 8. The committee agreed to remain until they completed the proposal and the engagement letter although some members had made other plans for the afternoon.

_____ 9. We think grammar should be taught, they think grammar should be eliminated.

_____10. Ned Kiriyama whom we selected as our department representative, asked each employee to complete the survey.

_____11. Although I prepared the report on time, the data and conclusions are not accurate.

_____12. Your budget report, I might say, is a good estimate of projected revenues.

_____13. The correct answers are: true for No. 5 and false for No. 7.

_____14. I will arrive on May 14; I need a car when I arrive.

_____15. Specifically, we need debugged, up-to-date software, and Molly Finch, our new systems manager, will select it.

_____16. Julie is the only non-member in attendance.

_____17. The exit report, that you prepared so carefully, was accepted by the committee.

1. C Commas are correctly indicated in the words that occur in a series, including the comma preceding the conjunction. (Rule 6)

2. I A comma is used between independent clauses joined by a conjunction. (Rule 1)

3. I A comma is needed between *clear* and *simple* because the two coordinate, parallel adjectives modify the same noun, *language*. (Rule 10)

4. C A semicolon is required before and a comma is required after a conjunctive adverb used to join independent clauses. (Rule 3)

5. C Dashes may be used to place emphasis on a part of the sentence or to provide needed content clarification. (Rule 9)

6. I A comma must follow *hand* to set off the introductory phrase. (Rule 7)

7. I *Above-mentioned*, as a compound modifier, must be hyphenated. (Rule 11)

8. I A comma should follow *letter* to indicate a desired pause before the dependent clause. (Rule 5)

9. I The sentence contains a comma splice. (LT2)

10. I A comma is needed after the proper name *Ned Kiriyama* to set off the complete appositive *whom we selected as our department representative*. (Rule 8)

11. C The comma correctly sets off the introductory dependent clause. (Rule 4)

12. C Commas correctly set off the internal sentence interrupter, *I might say*. (Rule 8)

13. I A colon is incorrect because it introduces a subject complement. If the colon is to remain, the sentence must read *answers are as follows:* . . . . (Rule 12)

14. C The semicolon correctly joins the two independent clauses. (Rule 2)

15. I A semicolon rather than a comma should be used after *software*. (LT5)

16. I *Non* is a common prefix that is seldom hyphenated. (LT17)

17. I *That you prepared so carefully* is an essential modifier that should not be set off with commas. To make the clause nonessential, the writer would have to replace *that* with *which*. (Rule 8)

PUNCTUATION EXERCISE 1   Name_____

Write *T* if the statement is true; write *F* if the statement is false.

_____ 1. Common coordinating conjunctions are *and, but, or, for, thus, hence,* and *yet.*

_____ 2. If a comma by itself is used to join two independent clauses, a run-on sentence results.

_____ 3. In general, a comma is used before *and* only when the *and* joins two independent clauses or joins items in a series.

_____ 4. In nearly every instance, the semicolon is used only when an independent clause both precedes it and follows it.

_____ 5. Most conjunctive adverbs are one-syllable words.

_____ 6. By itself, a dependent clause is not a sentence but is a fragment.

_____ 7. Typical subordinating conjunctions are *therefore, however, although,* and *nevertheless.*

_____ 8. In most instances, dependent clauses are formed when a subordinating conjunction is placed at the beginning of what would otherwise be an independent clause.

_____ 9. Dependent clauses that follow independent clauses are always set off by commas.

_____ 10. A series involves two or more items arranged in a sequence.

_____ 11. Writers who reflect a "comma-conjunction mentality" in their writing probably use a comma before most conjunctions.

_____ 12. In business writing, the comma is universally used before the conjunction in a series.

_____ 13. In business writing, short introductory phrases are typically **not** set off with commas.

_____ 14. Words such as *therefore* and *however* are used exclusively to join independent clauses.

_____ 15. An appositive is a pronoun; its antecedent is a noun that occurs earlier in the sentence.

_____ 16. Novice writers probably tend to use the dash too infrequently.

_____ 17. The cadence test is commonly used to determine whether a comma is used between two adjectives that precede a noun.

_____ 18. If you are introducing an enumeration and want to use a colon, you should be sure a complete sentence pattern precedes the colon.

PUNCTUATION   161

Write *C* to indicate the sentence is correct; write *I* to indicate the sentence is incorrect. Underline the subject of each clause once; underline the verb or verb phrase of each clause twice; and then bracket each dependent clause.

_____ 1.   He audited the books; but then realized he had made a mistake.

_____ 2.   We cannot assume such risks, therefore, we must choose another alternative.

_____ 3.   Most people use single entry bookkeeping to keep their checkbook balances up to date although accountants use double entry bookkeeping in their work.

_____ 4.   Specifically we must make certain all parts are in the proper order; otherwise the machine will not work properly.

_____ 5.   Three models that will be shipped are: 6W9, 17E2 and 21N4.

_____ 6.   The question is, fundamentally, economic; but serious political implications exist.

_____ 7.   The committee agreed to the proposal—one that few stockholders will accept.

_____ 8.   The long awaited tax bill just passed the Senate.

_____ 9.   The carefully-prepared report will be presented to the steering committee on Friday.

_____10.   The manuscript is scheduled for tomorrow it must be submitted in a folder.

_____11.   If we are to be totally prepared for the meeting we will need six copies of the agenda.

_____12.   The manager prepared a down-to-earth report that was short, and concise.

_____13.   The new software program is up-to-date in every detail.

_____14.   Luther prepared the report himself; but I presented the report to management.

_____15.   Every one of the members attended except: Ms. James, Mr. Kirk, and Ms. Morton.

_____16.   The software program worked fine yesterday, and appears to be working today.

_____17.   You must pick and choose among investments, the investment you choose will be a tradeoff between risk and return.

_____18.   The controller whose office is on the second floor is the person you need to see.

Write *A* if the first choice in parentheses is correct; *B* if the second choice is correct; and *C* if the third choice is correct.

_____ 1. Discounts are available (,/;) only buyers who pay cash, however, can qualify.

_____ 2. The bulletin was (short, interesting and very well written/short, interesting, and very well written).

_____ 3. A purchase order was sent to the (supplier, and/supplier and) the customer was told to expect shipment July 15.

_____ 4. We are looking for a (bright energetic,/bright, energetic/bright, energetic,) manager.

_____ 5. Our flight to (Atlanta, so I am told/Atlanta, so I am told,/Atlanta so I am told) will be delayed two hours.

_____ 6. The applicant has all the characteristics we are looking for (,/—/;) training, experience, initiative, and intelligence.

_____ 7. If the meeting is postponed until (Thursday, Mr. West/Thursday; Mr. West/Thursday Mr. West) will be unable to attend.

_____ 8. In a few instances (comma/no comma) the guidelines were completely disregarded.

_____ 9. Our Payroll Department promised to mail paychecks by the first of the (month and/month, and) to reimburse managers promptly for their travel expenses.

_____ 10. The boss approved our (proposal, however;/proposal; however,) we must raise additional funds before construction begins.

_____ 11. How much per yard is the (stain resistant/stain, resistant/stain-resistant) carpet?

_____ 12. The award will be given to (Mr. Taylor, our treasurer/Mr. Taylor, our treasurer,/Mr. Taylor our treasurer) for outstanding service.

_____ 13. John, Dan, and Kelly agreed to attend (,/;) but none of them, I am told, has paid his fees.

_____ 14. Give the assignment to Mrs. Preston (;/—) the one person we can count on!

_____ 15. The principles we discussed (are:/are as follows:) content, organization, and style.

_____ 16. X-Mart's (fast friendly/fast-friendly/fast, friendly) service is excellent.

PUNCTUATION EXERCISE 4   Name_____

Each sentence contains a semicolon. Mark *C* if the semicolon is used correctly; mark *I* if the semicolon is used incorrectly. Underline the subject of each clause once; underline the verb or verb phrase of each clause twice; and then bracket each dependent clause.

_____ 1. One calling card popular in Europe is making inroads here; you buy the card and make calls until you deplete its value.

_____ 2. Most cards provide a voice prompt; however, before and after each call.

_____ 3. Long-distance providers are very inventive in devising new features packaged into their cards; even new ways of placing calls.

_____ 4. For a call of a minute or two; a prepaid card is far less expensive than a calling card.

_____ 5. Technology has come up with an answer to the growing number of thefts of calling-card numbers; your voice.

_____ 6. The system isn't complete; although things look good for its being completed soon.

_____ 7. Each point is worth five frequent-flyer miles; and, as an added enticement, new customers get triple points the first month.

_____ 8. Quigley has the same deal; and is giving out 2,000 free miles to new customers.

_____ 9. Accumulate 100,000 points; then take a partner on a free three-night cruise to the Bahamas.

_____10. Someone with a similar voice who knows the password and the 800 number can call the system; as happened in a test with a customer's sister.

_____11. Most customers settle on a preferred long-distance provider; of course, to save money on their phone bills.

_____12. Quigley wants you to sign up for its service, however; and the inducements may convince you to do so.

_____13. Presently, the least-expensive time to call is over the weekend; Quigley hopes to provide those same rates during evening hours.

_____14. Quigley's weekly plan undercuts all competitors; but that advantage may not last long.

_____15. The ad campaigns don't tell you; moreover, that all long distance carriers raised their rates last month.

Edit to correct all punctuation errors. Two sentences contain no errors.

1. If we want additional service we must pay out of pocket costs.

2. Self-employed workers pay for their premiums but the premiums are tax deductible.

3. Under the plan some groups are big winners, the biggest winners are the working poor.

4. Nurses might be well informed, quality control officers; especially in hospitals.

5. The plan promises to: provide guaranteed benefits, and to safeguard health insurance.

6. Ron Spotten, small business owner in Moroni recommends a plan that is not up-to-date.

7. The less-expensive plan is the preferred-provider organization—requiring patients to go to specialized doctors.

8. With fee-for-service programs, competition—especially in rural areas—is becoming obsolete.

9. The public is aware of the costs of health care the public is ready for a change.

10. We want everyone insured, moreover we want employers to help pay employees' coverage.

11. The nation simply has too many people—30 million, without health-care coverage.

12. Services include immunizations, physicals, well baby care and cholesterol screening.

13. The plans when offered by alliances, will have a basic set of services as I mentioned above.

14. If in-patient services such as bed and board, and routine care are offered.

Edit to correct all punctuation errors. Two sentences contain no errors.

1.   Orrin wants more control-over-the-process, and thinks the governor has too much influence.

2.   Finally, Mr. Marks wants a bill to require near-instantaneous background checks for felons.

3.   The House passed Harmon's bill, the Senate is delaying debate on Lewis' bill.

4.   *Wasatch Magazine* is offering its subscribers an all expense paid three day trip to Jackson.

5.   Your application came at a good time although some parks—especially Zion, and Bryce, don't want the service.

6.   However, after the autopsy, we responded quickly—thinking the shooting may be accidental.

7.   Mr. Rex, head of the department found the package Mr. Ford confirmed it wasn't a bomb.

8.   Austin didn't know who sent the large, brown envelope so he called security.

9.   The Supreme Court ruled last year; however, that White could withdraw his plea.

10.   Therapists respond only when needed and they arrive within minutes.

11.   My speech according to Mindy caused you to cry even though you didn't understand.

12.   Shortly thereafter my mother, brother and sister emigrated.

13.   The two standard rules are: arrive on time, and put in a full day's work.

14.   When I entered the building I licked my lips, and tasted the chemicals.

INDEX

Coordinate modifier, 98, 102, 145, 155
Coordinating conjunction, 119-120, 123, 125, 145, 147, 149-150
Coordination, 119, 146-147, 155
Correlative conjunction, 119-120, 129

D

Dangling modifier, 99, 103-105
Dash, 125, 151, 154, 157-158
Dependent clause, 28, 38, 59, 99, 120-122, 125-126, 128, 144-145, 150-151, 153, *see* subordinate clause
Directions, 78-79
Direct object, 1-3, 9-10, 53, 58, 60, 83-85, 158
Double prepositions, 121, 131

E

Essential clause, 26, 38-39, 121, 126, 128-129, 153
Explanatory phrase, 31, 153-154
Expletive, 26, 39-40

F

Finding, 78-79
Fragment, 146, 150, 154
Future perfect tense, 51-53, 56-57, 61
Future tense, 51-53, 57-58, 60, 63

G-H

Gender, 27, 35-36
Gerund, 2, 4, 13-14, 53, 58
Helping verb, 5, 55, 77, 83, 85
Historical present, 53, 57, 59, 62, *see* literary writing, present viewpoint
Hyphen, 101-102, 108, 144-145, 155-157

I

If/then statement, 79-80, 129
Imperative mood, 76-82

Incomplete comparison, 99, 106
Indefinite pronoun, 26, 31
Independent clause, 59, 103, 120-121, 123-125, 128, 144-154, 157-158, *see* main clause
Indicative mood, 75, 77-79, 81-82
Indirect object, 1-3, 10
Infinitive, 1, 3, 11, 53, 56, 58, 62-63, 129
Intransitive verb, 53, 60, 83-85
Introductory clause, 104, 153
Introductory phrase, 128, 152-153
Introductory statement, 158
Introductory word, 152
Irregular verb, 51, 54-55, 83

J-L

Joint possession, 13
Linking verb, 4, 53, 82-86
Literary writing, 62, *see* historical present, present viewpoint

M

Main clause, 32, 33, 62, 99, 103-104, 122, 128, 146, *see* independent clause
Misplaced modifier, 97, 99-100
Modifier, 10, 26, 31, 53, 55, 58, 97-108, 144-146, 153-156
Modifiers chapter, 97
    Discussion, 97
    Terminology, 98
    Rules, 100
    Self-evaluation, 109
    Exercises, 111
Modifying phrase, 99, 103, 105
Mood, 52, 75-82, 86, *see* imperative mood, indicative mood, subjunctive mood
Mood chapter, 75
    Discussion, 75
    Terminology, 78
    Rules, 79
    Self-evaluation, 87

Exercises, 89

N

Nonessential clause, 26, 38-39, 121, 126, 128, 146, 153-154
Nonrestrictive clause, *see* nonessential clause
Noun, 1-5, 7-8, 10-14, 25-28, 33-39, 53, 58, 84, 97-99, 101-103, 129, 144-146, 154-157
Noun phrase, 38, 144
Number, 25, 27-28, 30, 32-36, 52-53

O

Object of an infinitive, 1, 11
Objective case, 1, 2, 6-7, 9-10, 14
Objective-case pronoun, 3-4, 7, 9-11
Object of a preposition, 1, 4, 7, 10-11, 27, 121

P

Parallelism, 119, 121, 123, 129, 132, 145, 155, *see* connective
Parentheses, 153-154
Parenthetical phrase *or* statement, 27, 31, 153-154
Participial phrase, 14
Participle, 52, 55-58, 61-62, 83, 85-86
Passive voice, 82-86, 105
Past participle, 52, 54-57, 61-62, 83, 85-86
Past perfect tense, 51-53, 55-57, 61
Past tense, 51, 54, 56-60, 62
Perfect infinitive, 62-63
Perfect participle, 62
Person, 27, 35-36, 52-53
Phrasal preposition *or* construction, 121, 130
Phrase, 2, 4-5, 10, 13-14, 27, 31, 34, 38, 55, 85, 97, 99, 103, 105, 119-121, 123-124, 128-129, 144, 146, 149, 151-153

Plural noun, 3, 11-12, 25, 27, 33-34, 36, 146
Plural possession, 3, 12
Plural pronoun, 25, 27, 36-37
Plural subject, 28-32
Plural verb, 25-30, 32-36, 52
Positive degree *or* form, 105, 106
Possession, 3-4, 12-13
Possessive case, 1-4, 11-14
Predicate, 83
Predicate adjective, 4-5, 8
Predicate noun, 1, 4-5, 8
Predicate pronoun, 1, 4-5, 8
Prefix, 157
Preposition, 1, 4, 7, 10-11, 14, 27, 31, 119-122, 130-132
Prepositional phrase, 4, 10, 14, 27, 31, 34, 122
Present infinitive, 56, 62-63
Present participle, 56-57, 62
Present perfect tense, 51-53, 56-57, 61, 63
Present tense, 51, 53, 56-60
Present viewpoint, 59, 62, *see* historical present, literary writing
Progressive tense, 52, 56-58
Pronoun, 1-14, 25-28, 31, 35-40, 84, 97-98, 103, 119, 123, 125-126
Proper adjective, 99, 102
Punctuation chapter, 143
    Discussion, 143
    Terminology, 144
    Rules, 147
    Self-evaluation, 159
    Exercises, 161

Q-R

Question, 2-3, 9-10, 30, 52, 75-79, 97
Recommendation, 75-76, 78, 80-81
Reference, 25, 27, 35-37
Reference chapter, 25
    Terminology, 25
    Discussion, 35
    Rules, 36
    Self-evaluation, 41

Exercises, 43
Referent, 35-36
Regular verb, 55, 57, 83
Relative clause, 28, 32-33, 38
Relative pronoun, 28, 32, 38-39, 119, 122, 125-126
Relatively permanent truth, 59
Request, 75-76, 80
Restrictive clause, *see* essential clause
Run-on sentence, 146, 148-149

S

Semicolon, 120, 123-125, 145, 147-150, 157-158
Sense verb, 86
Sentence interrupter, 146, 150, 153-154
Separate possession, 13
Series, 98, 102-103, 146, 149, 151-152
Shift in mood, 82, 86
Shift in tense, 57, 64, 86
Shift in voice, 86, 104
Simple tense, 52, 58
Singular noun, 3, 11-12, 25, 27, 32-36
Singular possession, 4
Singular pronoun, 25, 27, 29, 32, 34, 36
Singular subject, 27-31
Singular verb, 25-34, 52-53
Split construction, 122, 131-132
Statement of fact, 58, 75, 78-79
State of being, 5, 52, 56, 60, 86
State-of-being verb, 4-5, 8-9, 82-85
Subject, 1-5, 7, 9-11, 25-33, 35-36, 40, 53, 58, 76, 82-84, 86, 97, 99, 103-105, 123, 144-146, 153
Subject complement, 1, 4-5, 8-9, 83-84, 86
Subjective case, 1, 4-5, 7-9, 11
Subject of an infinitive, 1
Subjunctive mood, 75-78, 80-82
Subordinate clause, 59, 120, 122, 127-128, 145, 147, 150, *see* dependent clause

Subordinating conjunction, 119, 122, 128, 145, 150-151
Subordination, 119, 125
Suggestion, 75, 79
Superlative degree *or* form, 99, 105-106

T

Tense, 11, 51-64, 75, 81, 83, 86
Tense chapter, 51
    Discussion, 51
    Terminology, 52
    Rules, 58
    Self-evaluation 65
    Exercises, 67
Terminal preposition, 122, 131
That clause, 39, 153
Transition, 124, 146, 149, 152-153
Transitive verb, 58, 60, 83-84

U

Unit, 34, 36
Unit of measurement, 28, 34
Universal truth, 57-59

V-W

Verb, 1-5, 7-11, 13, 25-35, 39, 51-63, 75-86, 97-98, 107, 123, 129, 144-146, 148, 153, 157
Verbal, 53, 55, 58
Verb phrase, 5, 55
Voice, 52, 75, 82-86, 104
Voice chapter, 75
    Discussion, 82
    Terminology, 83
    Rules, 84
    Self-evaluation, 87
    Exercises, 89
Which clause, 39, 153